Emotional IQ

Master Your Emotions for Personal and Professional Success

Martha Loch

Table of Contents

Introduction...9

Part I: Discovering Your Emotional Self............. 14

Chapter 1: The Emotional Awareness Spectrum: Where Do You Fall?.. 15

The Emotional Awareness Spectrum......................... 16

Emotional Awareness Spectrum Self-Assessment Quiz 19

Chapter 2: Increasing Your Emotional Awareness 27

Why it is Necessary to Develop Emotional Awareness 27

Practical Exercise to Help Increase Emotional Awareness... 28

Chapter 3: Befriending Our Emotions to Enhance Emotional Awareness...35

Emotions Are Neither "Good" or "Bad"... They Just Are...37

Feelings Versus Actions 38

Own Your Feelings 39

Part II: Mastering Emotional Regulation 46

Chapter 4: The Neuroscience of Emotional Hijacking..47

Introducing Emotional Hijacking.............................. 49

Hacks to Avoid the Hijack.. 51

Chapter 5: Responding vs Reacting to Emotions 54

The Difference between Reacting & Responding 55

The Neuroscience of Reacting Vs. Responding..........56

Tips to Help You Learn to Always Respond Rather than React...57

Questions You Need to Ask Yourself Prior to Responding.. 60

Chapter 6: Cooling the Flames: Anger Management Essentials 63

Chapter 7: Lifting the Clouds: Coping with Sadness 72

Identifying the Root Cause of Your Sadness 73

7 Simple and Effective Ways to Help You Deal with Sadness 76

Chapter 8: Managing Fear and Anxiety.........................81

Understanding the Concepts of Fear and Anxiety 81

How Do I Help Myself? Coping with Fear and Anxiety 85

Chapter 9: The Surprising Upside of Negative Emotions 91

Part III: Cultivating Emotional Empathy........... 99

Chapter 10: The Empathy Advantage in Relationships 100

Why Empathy is Vital in Relationships 101

Simple Yet Practical Ways to Enhance Empathy in Your Relationships 104

Chapter 11: Walking in Their Shoes: Perspective-Taking as a Skill & How to Go About Practicing It 106

Understanding Perspective-Taking 106

Kinds of Perspective-Taking 107

Practicing Perspective-Taking – How to Go About It 109

Chapter 12: Perspective Taking: How to Teach this Social Skill to Kids 113

Chapter 13: When Empathy Backfires: Avoiding Emotional Burnout...120

Too Much of a Good Thing................................. 121

Confusing Charity for Empathy 122

Giving Too Much of Yourself 124

Part IV: Communicating with Emotional Intelligence 126

Chapter 14: Curing Emotional Tone-Deafness............ 127

The Two-Toned Conversation..................................128

Chapter 15: Assertiveness 101: Speaking Your Truth with Tact...133

Chapter 16: The Science of Conflict Resolution 139

Understanding Conflict Resolution 139

Resolving Conflict: A Step-by-Step Guide................140

Chapter 17: Talking Someone Down from an Emotional Ledge...149

On the Ledge...149

What Not to Do...150

What to Do..151

Part V: Applying EQ in Key Relationships........ 155

Chapter 18: Emotional Intelligence for Romantic Partners... 156

Benefits of EQ in Romantic Relationships 157

10 Ways to "Love Smart"..160

Chapter 19: Cultivating "True Friendships" via Emotional Intelligence 164

Chapter 20: Navigating Family Drama with Emotional Finesse 170

Tips and Strategies to Help You Resolve Family Conflicts..171

Chapter 21: EQ Essentials for Leaders and Managers 177

Part VI: Expanding Your Emotional Range 184

Chapter 22: Building Emotional Resilience 185

The 6 Traits of Emotional Resilience........................ 186

Exercises for Emotional Resilience 187

Chapter 23: Vulnerability: The Surprising Key to Emotional Strength 193

Understanding Emotional Vulnerability 193

Connected or Not: What Makes the Difference? 195

Daring to Connect: Steps to Embrace and Harness Vulnerability for Greater Emotional Strength and Better Relationships 197

What Vulnerability Is Not 199

Part VII: Lifelong Emotional Growth and Support 201

Chapter 24: Assessing Your Emotional Intelligence Progress 202

Chapter 25: Building a Strong Social Circle for Sufficient Emotional Support 209

5 Steps to Build a Strong Social Circle 209

Conclusion 215

Appendix... 216

The Emotional Intelligence Self-Assessment Test 217

Introduction

Do you often feel like stress, anxiety, depression, or anger are taking control of your life, or, at least, have way more influence over your reactions, responses and state of mind than you are comfortable with? Do you find yourself reacting impulsively all too often, often saying or doing things you almost always regret when everything has calmed down? Or – on the complete opposite end of the spectrum – are you prone to feeling emotionally detached or numb, even when the subject at hand has everyone else around you emotionally immersed and invested?

If your answer is yes to any or all of these questions, it could be an indicator that it's time to strengthen your *emotional intelligence (EQ)*.

What is Emotional Intelligence?

I like to define emotional intelligence (also known as EI or EQ, short for "emotional quotient") as the skill of *recognizing, interpreting, expressing, managing, evaluating,* and *utilizing* emotions to communicate and interact *effectively* and *constructively* with others. While the ability to express and control your own emotions is vital, equally important is the capacity to understand, interpret, and respond to the emotions of those around you.

Developing emotional intelligence will help you build stronger relationships, excel in school and work, and achieve your personal and career goals, among many other things. It will also enable you to *connect with your feelings*, *turn your intentions into actions*, and make well-informed decisions about what truly matters to you.

But with all this said, where did the term 'emotional intelligence' come from? Who coined it first?

Well, the term "emotional intelligence" was first introduced in a 1990 paper by Peter Salovey and John Mayer[i]. Their definition of it was "*a kind of social intelligence which involves the capacity to monitor your own as well as others' emotions and feelings, to "discriminate" among these feelings and emotions, and then use the information you get to guide your thoughts and actions.*" Their research, while a tad basic (compared to the volume of information in place today) owing to how new and unexplored the subject was, laid the foundation for our present understanding and appreciation of EI as a *set of abilities which contribute to not just effective interpersonal functioning but also personal well-being.*

Today, emotional intelligence is widely recognized as a very valuable skill set in personal development, education, leadership, workplace effectiveness, and a whole host of

other realms. So much so that some experts have even suggested that emotional intelligence is actually more important than IQ[ii] for success in life than IQ is.

Let's touch on this briefly.

Why Emotional Intelligence Matters More Than IQ

We are often taught that intelligence alone (or at least primarily) leads to success—think of all the movies you've watched or stories you've heard about people who excelled in academics and almost routinely carved a straight path to the upper rungs of wealth, recognition and success. But if you look really closely into these stories, you'll quickly realize that their achievements very often stem from another crucial factor: emotional intelligence.

Here are some of my top reasons why I believe EQ is the real key to success in life, and may actually be more important than IQ:

i) EQ has a bigger impact on success than all other factors. I have had many people argue with me that IQ will help you secure a job more than any other factor will. I always agree, and then raise the point that it's often a lack of emotional and social intelligence that leads to job loss. Most managers and workplace leaders agree that IQ only contributes only 20% to

your overall success, with the remaining 80% being influenced by your emotional and social intelligence.

ii) All too often, it is often *whom you know*, rather than what you know, that determines success. And nothing fosters healthy relationships quite like having a high EQ does. To maintain healthy relationships, we need to *understand our emotions, recognize their origins,* and *express them appropriately,* all of which are qualities and capacities synonymous with high emotional intelligence.

iii) Emotional health affects our physical health. This is not some willful extrapolation by the way: there is a clear link between our emotional well-being and our physical health[iii]. Chronic stress, which often stems from emotional discomfort, can lead to various health problems[iv]. It's estimated that over 80% of health issues are stress-related, which certainly highlights the importance of addressing our emotional health to improve physical well-being.

iv) Poor EQ has long been associated with criminal and unethical behavior[v]. It is very hard to discount or ignore the connection between inadequate emotional skills and increasing crime rates[vi]. From my many years working in the psychology and counseling field, I have found that it is those children with poor emotional skills who often become social outcasts, exhibit aggressive behavior, and struggle

academically. These challenges then lead to associations with others facing similar issues, which creates a pathway to criminal behavior.

With everything that you've picked up thus far, how can you expect this book to mold and transform your emotional landscape? Let's explore this in brief fashion.

How This Book Will Transform Your Emotional World

I have put together this guide to equip you with the tools necessary to both *understand* and *manage* your emotions more effectively. This book goes into detail on recognizing emotional triggers, which will help you gain control over reactions that may feel automatic or overwhelming at present. Once you allow yourself the time and patience to apply this newfound awareness, you will find that it's a lot easier to navigate complex social interactions and do so with more empathy and understanding than you were previously able to drum up.

And this will directly lead to cultivating a better relationship with others, and especially with yourself.

Let's get started without further ado.

Part I: Discovering Your Emotional Self

Chapter 1: The Emotional Awareness Spectrum: Where Do You Fall?

For the longest time, I wondered how so many intelligent, well-meaning people could often behave so poorly – even myself included. I mean, we understand the negative ramifications of acting out of turn, reacting rashly, getting into spats with others, etc. We understand that regardless of how unfair the situation is, it is always more constructive and beneficial to slow down, assess things, and respond in as calm and measured a manner as possible. We know these things. And yet, we often find ourselves doing the exact opposite.

As I started to conduct my own research and pick apart the litany of academic jargon, it slowly dawned on me that our emotional awareness has perhaps the biggest influence on how we react to situations, and how well-prepared we are for similar occurrences (and our reactions to them) in the future. Digging deeper, I found that there is a set emotional awareness *spectrum*, and our placement on it determines how we respond to things and situations, and how emotionally intelligent we are.

Let's unpack this in detail.

The Emotional Awareness Spectrum

I describe the *emotional awareness spectrum* as the *range of emotional sensitivity and recognition that you possess*, spanning from *basic awareness of emotions* to a more nuanced, more sophisticated understanding of the same.

There are 5 defined tiers of the emotional awareness spectrum:

Tier 5: This is the lowest end of the spectrum. At this point of the spectrum, there is limited emotional awareness, only being able to identify broad emotional states (happiness, sadness, anger, etc.) This basic awareness is very often tied to immediate, visceral reactions as opposed to a deeper understanding of the emotions' origins or implications. The vast majority of people do not fall here – this is pretty much reserved for very young children who are still too young for significant cognitive development or people with very severe mental health challenges and issues.

Tier 4: Emotional awareness becomes more refined as we move along the spectrum. You can recognize not only your emotions but also the triggers and patterns that cause them. You have also developed the ability to differentiate between similar emotions, which may have overlapping physical sensations but quite distinct psychological underpinnings (for example, between frustration and disappointment, or anxiety and excitement, etc.) Again, I have found from experience that most folks do not fall in this tier... you mostly have young children who've had some cognitive development, albeit not to a high enough level, and adults whose prior experiences or developmental challenges may have significantly compromised their emotional maturity.

Tier 3: Further along the spectrum, emotional awareness incorporates *an understanding of the complexity of emotions.* You are very capable of reflecting on your emotional experiences and recognizing exactly how multiple emotions coexist with and influence each other. For example, while you may feel both excitement and fear when starting a new job, you also understand why you're feeling both emotions all at once, as different as they are from each other. You're also significantly more adept at identifying the subtle shifts in your emotional state and understanding the context in which these shifts occur. Most people, I have found, fall in this tier... they have a significant level of emotional intelligence but are yet to deliberately work on refining and expanding on it to bump themselves up to the upper tiers (which this book will be useful for.)

Tier 2: This is the tier just directly below the highest level of the emotional awareness spectrum. At this tier, your level of emotional intelligence is undeniably high... you not only recognize and understand your own emotions but also readily empathize with others almost automatically. This level of empathy makes it really easy for you to properly perceive the emotions of those around you, *even when those emotions are not explicitly expressed*. To add to this, you are also able to consistently respond to others in ways that *acknowledge* and *validate* these emotions, which makes it very easy to cultivate deeper connections almost effortlessly and communicate effectively. I've found that the not-so-many people whom I categorize in this tier have all deliberately worked on improving their emotional intelligence at some point or other, which separates them from the rest of the pack.

Tier 1: This is the highest level. At this end of the spectrum, you're highly skilled in managing your emotions, and it is almost second nature for you to leverage your awareness to regulate any emotional responses you have in a healthy manner. You are also able to effortlessly harness your emotions to motivate yourself, cope with stress, navigate social environments, however complex they are, etc. This level of emotional awareness also involves a very "forward-looking perspective" – you are constantly anticipating how your emotions, and those of others, may/will evolve in all kinds of situations, which gives you the insight you need to act with both *foresight* and *sensitivity*. This is the level we all aspire to be and one that very few people actually manage to reach. And you know what the great news is? It isn't even difficult to reach it. If you consistently apply everything we explore and outline in this book, you will get there with no problem.

But as they say, in order to know where you are going, you must first understand where you are and where you're coming from. To get started on working to get to this level, you must first understand where you are on the spectrum.

Here is a quiz to help you determine this:

Emotional Awareness Spectrum Self-Assessment Quiz

This quiz is designed to help you assess where you fall on the emotional awareness spectrum. Answer each question as honestly as possible, and try and reflect on your typical behaviors and responses.

Question 1: When you experience an emotion, how easily can you identify what you're feeling?

A) I often struggle to pinpoint what I'm feeling and can only recognize very broad emotions (e.g., just knowing I'm "upset").

B) I can usually identify whether I'm feeling happy, sad, angry, or afraid, but not much beyond that.

C) I can recognize my emotions with some accuracy, and I often know whether I'm feeling frustrated, anxious, excited, etc.

D) I can easily identify the specific emotions I'm feeling, even when they are complex or mixed.

Interpretation:

If you chose A or B (quite unlikely, but definitely not impossible), you may be at the lower end of the spectrum, where emotional awareness is more basic. If you chose C or D, you likely have a more refined ability to identify your emotions.

Question 2: How well do you understand the triggers behind your emotions?

A) I rarely know why I feel a certain way; emotions seem to come out of nowhere.

B) Sometimes I can identify the reasons behind my emotions, but it's often unclear.

C) I usually understand what triggers my emotions, even if it takes some reflection.

D) I have a strong understanding of my emotional triggers and can often anticipate my emotional reactions to different situations.

Interpretation:

A or B suggests you may have limited insight into the triggers behind your emotions, indicating a more basic level of emotional awareness. C or D indicates a higher level of awareness, where understanding the origins of your emotions is more common.

Question 3: Can you differentiate between similar emotions?

A) I often confuse similar emotions and can't always tell them apart.

B) I sometimes struggle to differentiate similar emotions but can do so with effort.

C) I can usually tell similar emotions apart and understand the differences between them.

D) I easily distinguish between similar emotions and understand their distinct impacts on my behavior and thoughts.

Interpretation:

Choosing A or B suggests you're in the earlier stages of emotional awareness, where emotions might blend together. Choosing C or D reflects a higher level of sophistication in your emotional understanding.

Question 4: How well can you reflect on and understand the complexity of your emotions, especially when experiencing multiple emotions at once?

A) I find it difficult to understand or untangle complex emotions; they often just feel overwhelming.

B) I can sometimes reflect on my emotions and understand their complexity, but it's challenging.

C) I usually can reflect on and understand my complex emotions, recognizing when multiple emotions are at play.

D) I would say that I am skilled at identifying and reflecting on the complexity of my emotions, understanding how they interact and influence each other.

Interpretation:

A or B may indicate that you are still developing your ability to manage and understand complex emotional states. C or D suggests a more advanced capacity for emotional reflection and understanding.

Question 5: How well can you perceive and empathize with the emotions of others?

A) I often find it hard to tell what others are feeling unless they explicitly tell me.

B) I can sometimes guess how others feel, but I'm not always accurate.

C) I usually understand how others are feeling and can empathize with them, even if they don't say much.

D) I'm very attuned to the emotions of others and can often sense how they feel without them needing to say anything.

Interpretation:

A or B indicates that your emotional awareness might be more focused on yourself, with room to grow in recognizing others' emotions. C or D reflects a higher level of emotional intelligence, where empathy and understanding of others' emotions are well-developed.

Question 6: How effectively can you manage and regulate your emotions, particularly in stressful situations?

A) I often feel overwhelmed by my emotions and struggle to control them.

B) I sometimes manage my emotions well, but in stressful situations, I lose control.

C) I'm generally good at managing my emotions, even under stress, though it takes effort.

D) I have strong emotional regulation skills and can maintain control of my emotions, even in challenging situations.

Interpretation:

A or B suggests that you may be at the lower end of the spectrum in terms of emotional regulation, with room for growth. C or D indicates a strong capacity for emotional management, a sign of high emotional intelligence.

Question 7: How well can you anticipate your own and others' emotional reactions in different situations?

A) I rarely think about how I or others will feel in a situation until it happens.

B) I sometimes try to anticipate emotions, but I'm not always accurate.

C) I usually anticipate my emotional reactions and those of others, which helps me prepare for different situations.

D) I'm highly skilled at anticipating emotions in myself and others, which allows me to approach situations with sensitivity and foresight.

Interpretation:

A or B might indicate a more reactive approach to emotions, placing you on the earlier end of the spectrum. C or D suggests a more proactive and anticipatory approach, and shows a higher level of emotional awareness.

Scoring Your Quiz

1) Mostly A's: You may be at the basic end of the emotional awareness spectrum, where emotional awareness is still at the emergent phase (Tier 5).

2) Mostly B's: You have a developing emotional awareness, with genuine ability to understand and manage your emotions. (Tier 4).

3) Mostly C's: You demonstrate a solid level of emotional awareness and understanding. You're likely skilled in identifying and reflecting on your emotions, with room to refine these skills further (Tier 3, which is where most people fall.)

4) Mostly D's: You are at the high end of the Emotional Awareness Spectrum, exhibiting strong emotional intelligence. Your ability to understand, manage, and anticipate emotions is well-developed, and you likely navigate complex emotional landscapes with ease (Tiers 2 and 1).

With your understanding of the emotional awareness spectrum spruced up, chapter 2 explores increasing your emotional awareness.

Chapter 2: Increasing Your Emotional Awareness

"I just had this urge to throw something at the wall!"

"I just felt so bad in the moment!"

"I think he/she's just afraid to express their emotions, unlike myself."

These are a few examples of the responses I've received when asking my clients, "What do you feel about that?" This question is a crucial therapeutic tool, and for good reason. Our emotions, whether we realize it or not, often play a significant role in shaping our feelings, thoughts, and actions, which is why it is vital that we spruce up our emotional awareness.

Why it is Necessary to Develop Emotional Awareness

The emotions that arise within us significantly affect our relationships in the workplace and our personal lives. They shape how we live, influence our motivations, have an impact on how we allocate our time, and even have an influence on the careers we choose to follow. Essentially, our emotions play a starring role in guiding us in living a meaningful life.

If we're unaware of our emotions, we leave ourselves at their mercy. And without emotional awareness, we may very well end up living according to a script that we've never truly examined or understood and one that could end up leading us into a lot of trouble.

Being emotionally aware is vital for making decisions that truly serve our best interests. It affects how open we are to life, whether we allow ourselves to be vulnerable, take risks, stay curious, set and pursue our goals, and handle conflicts— both with others and within ourselves. For these reasons, the ability to *recognize, identify, accept,* and *understand* our emotions is vital for both our emotional and physical well-being.

Here are 5 steps that will help you vastly improve your emotional awareness.

Practical Exercise to Help Increase Emotional Awareness

Note: From my experience working with numerous clients, I have found that the exercise we're about to outline is most effective when applied on a daily basis, particularly at the end of the day when your day has all but unraveled and you've gone through varied experiences and situations. Feel free to examine the entire array of emotions that you may have experienced throughout your day... just ensure that you evaluate one emotion at a time. I would also recommend that you begin with the emotion you felt most intensely (frustration, anger, anxiety, etc.) and then work your way down the list.

Let's get started.

Step 1: The Cognitive Aspect of the Emotion

The cognitive aspect of an emotion involves *evaluating the event that triggered the emotion*—essentially, the "why" behind it. Think back to the moment when you felt the emotion. Can you recall what triggered it?

Ask yourself these questions:

i) How did the event differ from what you expected at the time?

ii) What were the chances that the event would result in negative (or positive) outcomes?

iii) How significant was the event to your goals or needs at that moment?

iv) Was the event caused by you or by someone else?

v) Could the event's consequences have been avoided or altered to your benefit?

Focusing on the "why" of the situation can provide valuable insights into what triggers these emotions for you. Identifying the trigger will enhance your emotional awareness, making it easier for you to anticipate future reactions and adjust your circumstances to encourage or prevent certain emotions.

Step 2: The Neurophysiological Aspect of the Emotion

Next, we need to consider the neurophysiological aspect, which includes the *physical symptoms you experience during emotions*. This is your body's way of preparing you for or alerting you to the event you're encountering. Reflect on how your body reacted when you felt that emotion.

Did you notice:

i) Skin becoming pale or flushed?

ii) Feeling cold shivers or warmth?

iii) Heartbeat slowing down or speeding up?

iv) Breathing slowing or quickening?

v) Muscles tensing or relaxing?

Not everyone experiences emotions in the same way. To enhance your emotional awareness, it will help to identify which emotions are associated with specific bodily responses. Being able to recognize these patterns will vastly improve your ability to accurately perceive the emotions you're experiencing.

Step 3: The Motor Expression Aspect of the Emotion

The next step is to explore the motor expression aspect of emotions, which involves the *changes in facial expressions, vocal tones, and body movements triggered by an emotion.* Essentially, this is how your body reacts to an event to express exactly what you're feeling. Think back to how your body language shifted in response to the event.

Did you:

i) Smile or frown?

ii) Move toward or away from people or objects?

iii) Make sudden movements or freeze in place?

iv) Open or close your eyes?

v) Raise or lower your voice?

vi) Speak assertively or with a trembling voice?

Understanding how you express your emotions through your voice and body language can enhance your emotional awareness, not to mention provide insight into how you present yourself to others. For example, do you raise your voice when angry, or do you become silent? Recognizing these behaviors allows you to ask yourself, "Is this how I want to express my anger?" This awareness will then help you gain control over your emotions and actively refine your outward behavior.

Step 4: The Motivational Aspect of the Emotion

The next aspect to consider is the motivational component of emotions. This involves the actions you take to focus your attention on the situation.

Reflecting on your experience, did you:

i) Shift your attention toward or away from the event?

ii) Focus on yourself or others?

iii) Physically move toward or away from the event?

Being aware of your automatic responses increases the likelihood of adjusting your behavior so that it suits the situation better.

Step 5: The Subjective Feeling Aspect of the Emotion

The subjective feeling aspect of our emotions is what makes *each emotional experience unique.*

Consider these questions:

i) How intense was the emotion?

ii) How long did the emotion last?

iii) Was the emotion positive or negative?

iv) How much arousal did the emotion create?

More importantly, think about why you experienced the emotion in that particular way:

i) Why was the emotion as intense as it was?

ii) Why did it last for the duration it did?

iii) Why did it feel good or bad?

iv) Why did it cause such a strong reaction?

You can then use this information to assess the significance of an event. For example, did you get angrier than expected when your coworker missed a deadline? Why do you think you reacted that way? Or, conversely, why didn't you get angrier? Reflecting on your emotions through this lens can help you compare your *current* situation with your *ideal* one.

Emotional awareness provides insight into how we are likely to experience an emotion in the future. Understanding this in advance helps us manage how we express our emotions. The more you practice this simple exercise, the easier it becomes. Try to incorporate it into your daily routine by reflecting on your day and using these steps to analyze different situations throughout your day. You will notice that your emotional awareness has vastly improved within a couple of weeks.

Up next, we explore the concept of befriending our emotions to further enhance our emotional awareness and intelligence.

Chapter 3: Befriending Our Emotions to Enhance Emotional Awareness

The vast majority of us didn't grow up with much guidance at all on how to understand or connect with our emotions. In fact, when I consult with my clients, it's clear that for most of them, discussions about emotions were often minimal.

Regardless, this does not mean that we didn't learn anything about them. In fact, we absorbed plenty of lessons. It's just that most of these were not consciously or deliberately taught. Rather, the messages that we received were shaped by unexamined beliefs and patterns, and they very likely continue to shape our (limited) view and perspective of emotions and how to deal with them.

Here are common lessons that we may have learned about emotions from a young age:

i) "Happiness" is good, while other emotions are bad.

ii) Emotions should be kept private or to ourselves.

iii) Expressing emotions openly is embarrassing or shameful.

iv) Experiencing strong emotions suggests we're "out of control," "unstable," or "weak."

v) Emotions are scary, dangerous, or inherently bad.

vi) Emotions need to be controlled, suppressed or managed.

vii) Emotions should be fleeting and mild; if they aren't, something is wrong with us.

viii) If we fully embrace emotions like sadness, anger, fear, grief, and fill-in-the-blank _____, we risk being overwhelmed and never recovering from them.

Our list could roll on and on, but I'm sure you catch my drift.

The majority of us were exposed to negative messages, as far as our feelings and emotions go, from a really tender age. These messages were often implicit, meaning they weren't directly stated. And because these implicit messages – along with the beliefs they create – are often veiled from our awareness, they're quite hard to challenge—we simply accept them as "the way things are."

Many of these harmful implicit messages were ingrained in our culture and passed down through generations, often rooted in trauma and the survival mechanisms that came with it. While I deeply understand and empathize with this, it is nevertheless time that we work on healing these "legacies" of inter-generational pain and trauma. And we can only do so by reshaping how we understand and relate to our emotions, and befriending them.

The very first step to take toward achieving this, is to understand that emotions "just are".

Emotions Are Neither "Good" or "Bad"... They Just Are

This is the very first thing that you must internalize if you are to completely overhaul your present view of emotions and how you deal with them and actually befriend them.

Emotions are simply energy in motion—e-motions, so to speak. They are energy moving through the body... nothing more. They aren't inherently good or bad; *they're just energy*. Like the weather, our emotions are always changing, with varying levels of intensity—sometimes strong and overwhelming, other times subtle and barely noticeable.

Letting go of the good/bad labels we've been taught to attach to our emotional states is the very first step toward developing a more mindful and accepting relationship with ourselves. The very first step here is to start taking note of the emotions and feelings that the inner critic within us labels as "bad." Which feelings and emotions most often trigger negative self-talk? Write these emotions down and repeatedly drill into your psyche to view them as not being bad every time they crop up, but rather as being mere energy in motion.

With this step done, the next crucial step is to distinguish between feelings and actions.

Feelings Versus Actions

It's crucial that we learn to distinguish between our feelings and our actions. Just because we experience an emotion doesn't mean we need to act on it. All feelings are valid and acceptable, no question about that... *but not all actions are.* For example, it's perfectly fine to feel angry, but it's not fine at all to take that anger out on others.

No feelings – not even the difficult and painful ones – present problems that need to be solved or eliminated. We often start believing that our emotions must be tightly managed and controlled—which is actually impossible—because we feel we have no choice in how we respond to our inner state. For example, if we think we have no option but to yell when we're angry, we mistakenly view *the anger itself as the problem to be fixed.* But really, it is the response itself that needs fixing... feeling angry, or upset, or whatever other emotion is okay. Responding by yelling or trashing the place isn't.

By befriending and building a relationship with our emotions, understanding that we don't have to feel compelled to act on them, and directing our efforts towards fixing our actions/reactions as opposed to our feelings; we greatly elevate our ability to tolerate uncomfortable feelings, which then opens up a range of possible (constructive) responses, if we even deem it fit to actually respond in the first place.

Once this step is in place, the next one is to own your feelings.

Own Your Feelings

In addition to being taught that emotions are bad, many of us were also taught that we are responsible for other people's emotions and vice versa. I have found that this belief often stems from weak emotional boundaries, where emotions weren't directly addressed or discussed. You may have been expected to guess how others were feeling by paying close attention to their body language, words, and actions. For instance, "Oh, mom is slamming doors and stomping around; she must be angry." Etc.

Taking full ownership of our emotions and being responsible for them is a very powerful and effective way to ensure that we're maintaining healthy emotional boundaries. Our emotions are ours to manage, and it's our responsibility to take care of ourselves and ask for what we need. The same applies to others—it's not our job to guess their feelings or "fix" them, and it's not their job to do that for us.

One of the most powerful lessons that I have learned over the years is that our emotions are constantly providing us with valuable information, be it about ourselves or those whom we associate with. If you frequently feel sad, angry, or rejected in your relationships, that's your body's way of signaling to you that something needs to change. Uncomfortable emotions often serve a specific purpose, and just because they're painful doesn't mean they're a problem. In fact, difficult, uncomfortable emotions are a very important feedback mechanism, often telling you what's okay and what isn't. We can learn to listen to these signals and take appropriate action in response (such as ending a relationship where you're constantly feeling unappreciated, calling workmates out when they saddle you with the bulk of responsibilities, etc.)

To wrap up, I want you to ask yourself the following questions. Think the answers through every question carefully and then write them down in the journaling space provided.

What Were You Taught About Emotions Growing Up?

What messages did your caregivers impart to you about emotions as you were growing up? What implicit lessons did you learn by observing others? What explicit messages did you receive directly? Which emotions were acceptable to express, and which were not? What narratives do you hold about emotions today?

_____

_____

_____

_____

_____

_____

_____

_____

_____

_____

_____

_____

_____

_____

_____

Emotional IQ

_____

_____

_____

_____

_____

_____

_____

_____

_____

_____

_____

_____

_____

_____

_____

_____

_____

What Is Your Relationship with Your Emotions Today?

Do you have a relationship with your emotions? If so, what is its nature? Is it one of care and compassion, or is it more critical and judgmental? Do you experience different types of relationships with various emotions? Are there certain emotions you go to great lengths to avoid? Are there emotions you're comfortable feeling, but only in private?

_____

_____

_____

_____

_____

_____

_____

_____

_____

_____

_____

_____

_____

_____

_____

_____

_____

_____

_____

_____

_____

_____

_____

_____

_____

_____

_____

_____

_____

_____

_____

_____

———————

Answering these questions will go a long way in helping you explore and understand your internal relationship with your emotions, which in itself will go a long way in helping you build trust in yourself. This self-trust will elevate your emotional awareness and enable you to handle *any* situation that life presents with a high level of confidence and emotional intelligence.

This chapter brings us to the end of Part I. Part II explores mastering emotional regulation.

Part II: Mastering Emotional Regulation

Chapter 4: The Neuroscience of Emotional Hijacking

It's universally acknowledged that the human brain is one of the most intriguing organs. This three-pound, jelly-like structure contains as many neurons as there are stars in the Milky Way. Mull over that for a bit. This three-pound mass of jelly also uses up roughly 20% (one-fifth) of the body's energy. That latter stat isn't all too surprising, however, when you consider that it is the body's command center, and plays the main role in enabling us to perform all of our daily activities.

However, it's far from perfect.

Among all the amazing things our brain can do, its top priority is keeping us alive. This means that it's constantly on the lookout for anything it perceives as a threat to our survival. Back in the caveman era, threats were straightforward—animals, harsh weather, encounters with other cavemen, you name it. The brain's response was equally simple: it assessed emotional cues to determine if a situation was pleasant, unpleasant, or neutral, then prompted us to either approach it, avoid it or merely ignore it.

This process still makes sense today in some situations. For instance, if you encountered a bear or a lion, the initial emotional response that you would have would be fear/trepidation, signaling your brain that the situation is unpleasant and that you must avoid it at all costs. Your brain would then prepare your body to either fight the threat or flee, raising your heart rate to send more blood to your muscles and brain, increasing your breathing for more oxygen, and shutting down non-essential functions to conserve your energy and focus.

But what about when a car cuts you off in traffic, your mother-in-law criticizes your parenting, or someone tells you that skinny jeans, which you love dearly and have dozens of pairs of in your closet, are out of style? Your heart starts racing, your breathing quickens and it becomes all you can think about—sound familiar? This happens because, as we've evolved, our brains have stuck with the same tried-and-tested process of assessing if the situation is pleasant, unpleasant, or neutral, then prompting us to respond appropriately, even though our lives have since become way more socially complex compared to the caveman days of our ancestors.

As a result, our brain doesn't always distinguish between actual physical threats and emotional reactions, which brings us to the subject of emotional hijacking.

Introducing Emotional Hijacking

To understand emotional hijacking, it's important to know two key components: the amygdala (which processes emotions) and the prefrontal cortex (which handles reasoning and thinking).

In the event of an 'emotional hijack', the amygdala essentially overrides the normal reasoning mechanism and process of the prefrontal cortex to take control of a situation. While the term "hijack" may sound severe, it's not always a bad thing. In a genuine emergency, like the bear encounter mentioned earlier, you wouldn't want your brain to waste time analyzing every possible reaction and debating the most logical course of action. Instead, you would need to act as quickly and efficiently as possible, which is why the amygdala steps in and triggers the fight-or-flight response.

The challenge arises when the amygdala takes over in non-emergency situations (such as our earlier examples of your parent-in-law criticizing your parenting style, a friend critiquing your beloved skinny jeans, etc.) During an emotional hijack, our rational thinking becomes paralyzed—

our IQ drops, our ability to make complex decisions diminishes, we lose the capacity to consider other perspectives, and our memory may even suffer. This, as you might guess, isn't exactly helpful in social situations, especially when you consider these situations are far from being emergency ones, even though your brain triggers responses as though they are.

However, even though our fight-or-flight response is deeply embedded in us through evolution, it is possible to override it. And you can do so by understanding and applying particular hacks to avoid the hijack. Once you apply these hacks for long enough, they will come as second nature, and as simple as they are, they will completely transform your emotional landscape and how you respond to unpleasant situations (particularly those that are non-emergency, which make up the bulk of the uncomfortable situations we encounter).

Let's explore these hacks.

Hacks to Avoid the Hijack

Here are four simple brain hacks to help you pause your emotions and return to logic and reasoning:

Hack #1 — Identify the Emotion

Naming/identifying the emotion is the first hack. Simply recognizing and naming what you're feeling can instantly shift you back into your rational mind. This requires pausing, analyzing, and using language—all of which are functions of the prefrontal cortex, which we explored earlier in this chapter. I have observed that even saying something as simple as "I am so mad" can significantly lessen the intensity of the emotion and coax you back to a more logical state.

Hack #2 — Change Your Environment

Switching up your environment is the second hack. Just like naming your emotions, getting up and moving around instantly forces you to consider your surroundings, which reengages the thinking parts of your brain that were momentarily shut down. This has the ultimate effect of steering you back to a more logical, rational state.

Hack #3 — Solve a Quick Math Problem

The third hack is to solve a quick math problem. Even a "problem" as basic as counting to ten will suffice. Or, you can perhaps do some basic calculation and division problems if you would like to engage your brain some more. Doing a simple math problem in your head not only jumpstarts your rational thinking but also briefly distracts you from the source of your emotional response.

Hack #4 — Share the Burden

The fourth hack is to *share the burden*. One thing I have discovered (and marveled at) is that when I hike up a hill with someone else, I perceive the hill as less steep than when I hike alone. I have asked countless other people if the same is true for them, and they've all responded in the affirmative. The same principle applies to emotions. When you share your feelings with a trusted friend or partner, you effectively split the mental burden, and this makes the situation feel less overwhelming and helps your brain feel less threatened.

To wrap up, all of these hacks on their own will be effective. But I often recommend that you combine them all for an even greater, swifter "jolt" back to logical and rational thinking, especially when a non-emergency situation has nevertheless left you very rattled and bothered. It shouldn't take you much time to chain these hacks together, too... each one of these hacks will cost you several seconds at best. Once you have enough practice applying these hacks to stave off emotional hijacking, you will quickly realize that your emotional awareness, and thus emotional intelligence, increase.

Up next, we explore responding to versus reacting to emotions.

Chapter 5: Responding vs. Reacting to Emotions

When someone says or does something that upsets us, our first instinct is often to *react* immediately and express how we feel. After all, they've upset and hurt our feelings, so we feel there's a need to immediately let them know they've done so, or perhaps even get them back. They deserve it anyway, right?

However, when emotions are intense, these reactions may not be as constructive or kind as we'd like them to be, at least in the long term. While reacting might feel satisfying in the moment (and it often does, let's be honest), allowing our emotions to settle and responding from a more balanced state will always lead to better outcomes in our relationships. In fact, it is very, very rare that the outcome is better when we react immediately, as opposed to when we bide our time and actually respond. This brings us to the question – what is the difference between reacting and responding?

Let's explore this.

The Difference between Reacting & Responding

Here is the primary difference between reacting and responding:

A *reaction,* oftentimes, is *swift* and *emotional.* This is perhaps the best and most straightforward metric to use when determining if your actions or words constitute a reaction. A lot of the time, it is driven by immediate feelings rather than thoughtful, painstaking assessment and consideration. It is usually *automatic, impulsive,* and shaped by past experiences and subconscious influences. Reactions can sometimes result in unintended—and often negative— consequences. For example, if a person says something that upsets us, we may snap back without thinking, which may escalate the situation further.

In contrast, a response is more *thoughtful, intentional,* and guided by higher emotional intelligence. It involves taking a moment to carefully assess the situation, reflect on what we're feeling and why, and then consider the potential outcomes. Responding, at its core, means choosing a course of action that aligns with our goals and leads to a more positive resolution.

Let's glean a little into the neuroscience of reacting versus responding.

The Neuroscience of Reacting Vs. Responding

Varied areas of the brain are engaged during reactions versus responses. When we're reacting, the more primitive part of the brain – the amygdala – which handles emotions, quickly takes control. This area doesn't focus on rational thinking or long-term consequences... rather, it focuses on immediate survival and swift reactions to perceived threats. In contrast, when we respond, the prefrontal cortex—responsible for decision-making and social behavior—takes charge. This part of the brain allows us to evaluate options, consider consequences, and make decisions based on logic rather than emotion. Since we explored these aspects of the amygdala and prefrontal cortex in quite some depth in our subject of emotional hijacking, there is no need to delve more into this. Nevertheless, it was necessary to make the correlation.

Up next, we explore tips to train yourself how to always respond instead of react.

Tips to Help You Learn to Always Respond Rather than React

You can greatly enhance your interactions with others and improve your personal well-being by learning to respond thoughtfully rather than reacting impulsively. Incorporating these practices into your daily routine will boost your communication skills and better equip you to handle stressful situations.

Tip #1: Pause & Breathe

A basic yet effective technique that I have found to help greatly in responding, as opposed to reacting, is to give yourself a brief pause whenever you're feeling overwhelmed/emotionally charged. If possible, close your eyes and take a few deep breaths. This can help slow down the physical sensations of stress, and give your mind the split-second moment it needs to catch up before you speak or act. This pause can turn a potential overreaction into a more measured response. So, before speaking/acting on something unpleasant someone else said or did, take a moment to pause, breathe, and settle into your body before responding.

Tip #2: Reflect Before Speaking

Before responding, take a moment to think about what you want to achieve. Will an immediate reaction help you reach this goal? Reflecting allows you to align your actions with your objectives, which will almost always lead to a more purposeful and constructive response.

I'm also a big proponent of practicing "kind communication," speaking with empathy and kindness, regardless of how slighted we are, or perhaps even how malicious the other party is in their words or actions. Whatever the goal may be, I have found that practicing kind communication in your responses often makes a significant difference, instantly diffusing charged situations and making malicious parties immediately question their actions and the merits behind the same. "Killing them with kindness" actually works.

Tip #3: Practice Active Listening

Fully understanding the other person's perspective is crucial for responding effectively. Engage in active listening by giving your full attention to the speaker. Consider their words carefully and avoid planning your response while they're talking... just listen to listen, as opposed to listening to answer back. This approach helps you respond more thoughtfully and also makes the other person feel heard and respected, which can help prevent conflicts.

Tip #4: Identify Your Triggers

Everyone has specific triggers—situations, words, or behaviors that elicit a strong emotional response. Try to pinpoint the situations where you tend to react emotionally and explore what might be triggering you. Being aware of these triggers can help you feel more prepared to manage them calmly when they occur, and allow you the time and mental space to choose a more thoughtful response. Also, make a habit of labeling your emotions after being triggered (for example, "I am angry/flustered/anxious/worked up, etc.) to gain even greater awareness of the causative elements that bother and trigger you.

Tip #5: Use 'I' Statements

When responding, express your thoughts and feelings by starting sentences with "I" instead of "you." For example, say, "I feel upset when" rather than "You make me upset." This approach focuses on your personal experience rather than blaming or accusing the other person (you may not even mean to blame them, but it's very possible that they'll take it that way.) This will help foster a more constructive, less confrontational conversation.

With these tips down, let's look at 5 questions you need to ask yourself before responding, to further anchor and bolster your capacity to actually respond, as opposed to reacting.

Questions You Need to Ask Yourself Prior to Responding

Developing a habit of responding thoughtfully will help foster more constructive and empathetic interactions. In moments of potential conflict or stress, asking yourself a few key questions can help shift your mindset from being reactive to taking a more compassionate approach.

By considering these questions, you encourage yourself to *pause, thoroughly evaluate the situation,* and then *choose your response carefully.* Doing so will help to minimize misunderstandings and strengthen your relationships with others.

Here are the questions:

Question #1: What am I feeling right now?

Take a moment to acknowledge your current emotional state. Identifying your feelings will help you understand what your immediate reaction may reveal about your subconscious and why a situation may be affecting you so strongly. This awareness can guide how you address these emotions in your response.

Question #2: What outcome do I hope to achieve?

Think about what you ultimately want from the interaction. Whether your goal is to resolve a conflict, communicate a point, or offer support, keeping the desired outcome in mind will help you align your responses with your objectives.

Question #3: How can I express my feelings constructively?

Consider how you may communicate your feelings and emotions in a manner that is both *honest* and *respectful*. The goal here is to share your thought process with *calmness* and *clarity* to prevent the situation from escalating.

Question #4: What could the opposite party be feeling/needing?

Try to empathize with the other person/party involved by considering what they may be feeling or needing. This perspective can help you tailor your response to be more sensitive and effective in addressing *both of your needs*.

Question #5: Is there more information I need before responding?

It helps to recognize that the urge to react quickly can sometimes (well, oftentimes) lead to misunderstandings. Reflect on whether you have all the necessary information to make an informed response. If you're uncertain, it's okay to ask questions or take time to gather more details.

When you learn to respond, as opposed to reacting, you become more adept at diffusing potentially problematic situations before they even happen and are able to foster stronger relationships with others, all of which are hallmarks of an emotionally intelligent person.

Up next, we explore the essentials of anger management.

Chapter 6: Cooling the Flames: Anger Management Essentials

Do you often feel like your anger is out of control? Perhaps, you've tried different approaches to manage it, but absolutely nothing seems to work. If this describes you, the thing is – you're not alone. Not at all. There are millions and millions of people just like you, struggling with the same things as you are.

As a counselor, I've spent years helping people who struggle with anger. Over time, I've discovered a few fundamental principles that everyone needs to know to manage their anger effectively. I came up with what I call the "*5 Essentials of Anger Management*" to help you understand what's necessary to change how you handle anger. These refined essentials are the result of hundreds and hundreds of hours spent studying anger and working with real people. If you've had difficulty controlling your anger, applying these 5 essentials will completely revise how you deal with and control it.

Let's get right into it.

Anger Essential # 1 – Anger & Responsibility

No one can "make you" feel angry. Through my years as a counselor, I've learned that the key to successful anger management isn't related to a person's personality, gender, or income. The real determinant of your success in managing anger is your ability to take responsibility for your own *thoughts, feelings,* and *emotions.*

You might be asking why this is one of the 5 essentials of anger management. The reason is simple: no one has the power to make you feel angry. You may perhaps have said things along the lines of, "They make me so mad when they do that!" But ask yourself: "Can anyone truly force me to feel a certain way? Can they really?"

If you believe they can, then you're giving others direct power and control over your emotions. Whoever they are – your spouse, children, coworkers, a stranger on the road, etc. – you're allowing them to dictate your feelings, which is quite absurd if you think about it. Anger management, at its core, is about reclaiming control over your own thoughts, emotions, and actions. So, to effectively manage your anger, the first step is to recognize how you've been relinquishing your power to others. Then, you can draw the line and ensure that this doesn't happen again (or at least happens less and less every time.)

Anger Essential # 2 – Anger & Your Emotions

Earlier in the book, we stressed that there are no "bad" emotions. And the same applies to anger. Anger is in no way a negative emotion. In fact, anger is a very fundamental human emotion. Many people struggle with anger not because it is bad, but because they don't fully understand it or how it functions.

When I work with people on anger management, I first emphasize that the goal isn't to eliminate anger *but to alter your relationship with it*. It's crucial to understand that anger itself isn't inherently bad. If you view anger as a negative emotion, you may avoid, fear, or even disregard it, leading to more problems. Anger only becomes problematic when it occurs too frequently or becomes excessively intense.

To regain control over this emotion, it's important that you express anger *appropriately* and *in the right contexts*. And how do you do so? The biggest leap you'll take towards this dynamic is to apply the advice and tips we explored on learning to respond instead of react in the previous chapter.

Try and always think of anger as a pendulum swinging between two extremes: avoiding anger on one side and experiencing excessive intensity on the other. The objective is not to ignore or let anger become uncontrollable... it is to maintain a healthy balance between these extremes.

Anger Essential # 3 – Anger & Your Body

Calming your body can help manage your anger. But let's track back a little...

Anger often manifests physically; you may feel your heart racing, your muscles tensing, your face heating up, etc. There's a strong link between your physical state, your mind, and your emotions. By paying attention to and regulating your body, you can completely influence your anger, and how you channel it.

One effective method that I have found for reducing anger by calming the body is the "body scan" technique. This technique can help you identify anger "in your body" and subsequently alleviate its physical symptoms. Try practicing this technique daily when you're not feeling upset, so you are able to apply it effectively during moments of anger.

Here's how to go about it:

1. Find a comfortable seated position with your feet flat on the ground. Rest your hands on your lap or the arms of your chair, with your palms facing upward.

2. Take a slow, deep breath in through your nose. Hold your breath briefly, then exhale slowly through your mouth.

3. Repeat this process for five slow, deep breaths.

4. Gently close your eyes and mentally scan your body from head to toe.

5. Focus on each muscle group individually, noting where you feel tension.

6. When you identify a tense area, take a slow breath and work on releasing the tension in that part of your body.

7. Observe how your body feels and changes after this process.

Anger Essential # 4 – Anger & Your Mind

The other essential skill to develop in relation to managing your anger is managing your thoughts. I always tell my clients that anger is triggered by how they perceive situations, *not by the situations themselves*. It's not what happens to you, *but how you interpret it* that causes your anger. As such, you must manage your thoughts first, to be able to manage your anger effectively. Developing this skill requires tons of practice, seeing as how your thought patterns have formed over many years and are very unlikely to change overnight. I have also studied that the vast majority of people who struggle with anger often have "unhelpful thinking patterns" that contribute to their frustration. See if you can recognize some of these patterns in your own self. If you do, double down even harder on learning to respond, instead of reacting:

i) Black & White Thinking: You often view situations in absolute terms, seeing things as either all good or all bad with no middle ground.

ii) Mind Reading: You're prone to assuming that you know what others are thinking or what they intended to convey, oftentimes without verifying it first.

iii) Labeling: You're prone to assigning negative labels to others, which often fuels your anger towards them (for example, calling someone a "jerk", or assuming someone's political affiliation means they're "an idiot.")

iv) "Should"ing or "Must"ing: You're prone to becoming frustrated with yourself for not meeting your own standards, or with others for not behaving according to your expectations.

Anger Essential # 5 —Anger & Understanding Its Stages

This far down the essentials list, you've for sure begun to see and acknowledge the key relationship between your thoughts, emotions, and body when experiencing anger.

I've found it very useful to view anger as a spectrum *ranging from 0 to 10*, rather than a simple on/off state. As your anger increases, it becomes more intense and considerably harder to manage. Consider how your feelings of anger shift at different levels, like, say, at level 3 versus level 7. Observe how your body responds and how your thoughts evolve as your anger intensifies. Recognizing these stages of anger is crucial for effectively managing and controlling it.

Here is my personally derived anger spectrum. See if you can apply it in your own psyche:

Level 1: Calm: Feeling relaxed and unaffected by stressors or provocations, maintaining a state of peace and composure.

Level 2: Aroused: Noticing a heightened sense of awareness or alertness, with mild emotional tension beginning to build.

Level 3: Stirred: Experiencing a noticeable increase in emotional agitation, with growing discomfort or unease.

Level 4: Frustrated: Facing challenges or obstacles that cause significant irritation and a sense of being blocked or thwarted.

Level 5: Irritated: Feeling a persistent annoyance or displeasure due to ongoing minor issues or disruptions.

Level 6: Angry: Exhibiting clear signs of emotional agitation and dissatisfaction, with a more intense reaction to provocations.

Level 7: Worked up: Reaching a heightened state of emotional disturbance, where agitation becomes more pronounced and difficult to manage.

Level 8: Irate: Displaying strong, intense anger with overt expressions of frustration and agitation.

Level 9: Vicious Crazed: Experiencing extreme and uncontrollable rage, with erratic behavior and a loss of rationality.

Level 10: Violent: Exhibiting severe and harmful aggression, where anger leads to physical or emotional harm directed towards others or yourself.

This chapter has shown you how to cope with anger by understanding and applying the five essentials of anger management. Up next, we explore how to cope with sadness.

Chapter 7: Lifting the Clouds: Coping with Sadness

Sadness is a natural part of life, we all know this. But the fact that we understand this doesn't make it any easier to manage the sorrow and unhappiness that you may be feeling. Nevertheless, I like to tell my clients that whether they are facing disappointment or experiencing deep grief, they should take comfort in knowing they're not alone and that even the most accomplished, well-put-together people they know wrestle with bouts of sadness themselves. And constantly too. Most importantly, I like to insist to my clients that the pain they may be feeling at present, however heavy, is only temporary.

Years and years of counseling clients has taught me two things about coping with sadness: one, to be able to truly cope with sadness and stave it off, it is crucial that you first identify the root cause of your sadness. It's quite difficult to deal with sadness – or any other emotion – without knowing its causative elements first. Two, KISS – keep it simple sir – insofar as simple ways to deal with sadness work best. I have found that having long-winded ways to deal with sadness often works poorly because when you're dealing with sadness, the bouts often come in so suddenly and quickly, and you need equally swift and simple ways to offset the sadness before it truly takes root and takes over your mind. As such, the ways and methods that I recommend here will all be really simple, and ones that you can apply in a matter of seconds to minutes.

But first, let's start with identifying the root cause of your sadness.

Identifying the Root Cause of Your Sadness

We all experience sadness sometimes, but the reasons behind it can vary. Sadness can stem from many different sources, and two people may react differently to the same situation.

If you're feeling sad, it could be due to a variety of factors:

i) Relationship Challenges:

Our connections with family, coworkers, friends, and romantic partners can evoke a range of emotions. You might feel sad because someone you care about hurt you, because you miss how a relationship used to be, or because a relationship has ended. Sadness in these situations can often be accompanied by feelings of loneliness. If your sadness is accompanied by feelings of loneliness, it is a good indicator that it may stem from relationship challenges.

ii) Personal Loss:

Any form of loss can lead to sadness—whether it's the loss of a cherished item/possession, missing out on a job opportunity, going through a divorce, moving to a new place and leaving your support system behind, grieving the loss of a loved one, etc. It's common to experience sadness and grief after any kind of loss, especially when it involves death. In addition to sadness, grief from a death might also bring feelings of guilt or anger. If your sadness is accompanied by feelings of guilt or anger whose reason you can't quite pin down, it is a good indicator that it may stem from losing someone you loved, even though may believe that you've since gotten over it.

iii) Unhealthy Thought Patterns:

Negative thought patterns such as self-criticism, overgeneralization, obsessive thinking, and excessive jealousy can shape how you perceive your experiences. When you're inclined toward negative thinking, you're more likely to view events negatively, which can contribute to feelings of sadness.

iv) Depression:

Feeling sad doesn't necessarily mean you're depressed, but persistent sadness is a key symptom of clinical depression.

Depression can make you feel sad without a clear cause and is often accompanied by other symptoms such as *fatigue, loss of appetite,* and *irritability.* Keep an eye out for these symptoms if you're prone to persistent bouts of sadness. Fortunately, there has been a massive evolution in depression and its handling over the past decade, and there are various treatment options available for managing depression. So, don't hesitate to seek help from a mental health professional if you think you might be depressed.

v) Stress:

Stress often leads to feelings of anxiety or anger. However, it can also result in sadness, particularly in cases of chronic stress—ongoing, relentless stress without relief. Over time, this can lead to burnout and even major depressive disorder (MDD).

No matter what's causing your sadness, there are effective ways to manage it. I'll say that from my experience as a counselor, coping strategies vary from person to person, so don't be discouraged if it takes some time to find the best approach for you. With this said, here are eight simple and effective strategies for dealing with sadness that I have found work seamlessly for most of my clients dealing with sadness.

7 Simple and Effective Ways to Help You Deal with Sadness

Before we get into the ways to help you deal with sadness, I would like to point out something critical, first: There are many ways to cope with sadness, but not all are healthy. I know it can be tempting to use self-medication or other harmful methods to numb or avoid painful feelings, but do understand that these approaches will do nothing to help you address the root of your sadness. As we've just explored, this is essential for moving forward, and why it's crucial that you find healthy and constructive ways to manage your sadness.

So, stay away from drugs/self-medication, self-harm, and other ways which you know, deep down, are harmful. They may numb your pain for a while, but that'll wear down, and you'll still have the same issues to deal with.

If you're feeling down, first find the root cause of your sadness... we've already explored this subject. Then, apply the following simple yet effective coping strategies. They can help you process your emotions and improve your mood:

1) Allow Yourself to Feel Sad

I have found that resisting your emotions by bottling them up or ignoring them will only make things worse over time.

Instead, acknowledge and accept your sadness. Just that. If crying helps relieve stress and sadness, don't hold back—let yourself cry if you need to and feel no shame about it whatsoever.

2) Prioritize Basic Self-Care

When you're feeling unhappy, taking care of yourself can be quite challenging, but neglecting your basic needs, like sleep and a healthy diet, can worsen your mood. Self-care – particularly basic self-care – is essential for validating and acknowledging your emotions. Research even suggests that small things, like what you eat, can directly affect your mood[vii]. So, if you're feeling particularly down, taking ten minutes off and having a nutrient-rich meal may instantly boost your energy and lift your spirits. Or, if you reckon you haven't been sleeping enough, you may find that sprinkling your day with small naps greatly improves both your mood and overall energy levels.

3) Steer Clear of Unhealthy Coping Mechanisms

While indulging in junk food, impulsive shopping, or alcohol/drugs might provide temporary relief, these destructive behaviors only offer short-term comfort and never, ever address the underlying issues. Focus on recognizing unhealthy coping mechanisms in your life, whatever they may be, and supplanting them with healthier alternatives, such as the ones we're outlining here.

4) Reach Out to Loved Ones for Support

An essential aspect of coping with sadness is recognizing when to seek help, which I recognize can sometimes be challenging, especially when you're feeling down and don't really want to be around people, let alone speak on the issue that is bothering you. However, friends and family can offer the love and support you need during tough times. They may not even understand your problem or provide helpful feedback, but the very act of them giving you a listening ear can massively offset your sadness.

5) Spend Time with Your Pet

While spending time with others can be comforting, you don't always need human company to feel better. Playing with your pet or taking them for a walk can instantly boost your mood. If you don't have a pet, consider volunteering at an animal shelter. Research shows that animals can alleviate symptoms and signs of depression[viii], and volunteering is yet another proven and practical way to lift your mood and combat loneliness, depression, and anxiety.

6) Find a Healthy Outlet for Your Feelings

Expressing your emotions, whether positive or negative, is absolutely crucial. However, expressing your emotions in unhealthy ways, such as throwing cutlery at the wall or slamming doors will only exacerbate the issue, so do avoid these. Instead, engaging in activities like art projects, journaling, or any other creative outlets that you enjoy can help you process and understand your sad feelings better.

7) Seek Out Opportunities to Laugh

When you're feeling off, laughter may seem out of reach. However, it is indeed true that laughter "is the best medicine." Research shows that consistent laughter has a positive psychological impact. It can be hard to laugh in moments of sadness, but even a smile can start to lift your mood. Watch your favorite comedy show, spend time with a funny friend, listen to a stand-up comedian, etc. Whatever makes you laugh, try and access it. Once you start laughing, you'll find that it becomes very difficult to keep feeling sad.

All of these are very simple and straightforward ways to deal with sadness. And this is what makes them so effective. Bouts of sadness often come on so suddenly and quickly, which calls for swift, easy-to-apply remedies to keep it at bay.

Up next, we explore managing fear and anxiety.

Chapter 8: Managing Fear and Anxiety

Understanding the Concepts of Fear and Anxiety

Fear is one of the most potent emotions, and it often exerts a significant impact on both mind and body. It is, however, a crucial human response that plays a vital role in our survival, helping us react to emergencies or dangerous situations like fires, life-threatening attacks, etc. However, owing to how our brains have been wired over thousands of years (we've already explored this, both in the emotional hijacking and reaction vs. responding chapters), fear can also arise in everyday, non-life-threatening situations (exams, public speaking, job interviews, dates, social events, et al.) It's a natural response to situations that put you under pressure.

Anxiety, on the other hand, is the term we use to describe *fears related to the possibility of something going wrong in the future*, rather than an immediate threat. Anxiety can be temporary, passing once the situation causing worry is resolved, but it can also persist and greatly interfere with daily life. Prolonged anxiety can impact our ability to sleep, eat, or focus, and it can prevent us from genuinely enjoying life... sometimes it can get so bad that it can even stop us from leaving the house for work or school.

When anxiety keeps you from doing the things you want or need to do, it can negatively affect your health. I have had clients who'd become so overwhelmed by fear that they started avoiding *any and all* situations that could trigger their anxiety... even basic activities like going out for food and groceries.

Breaking this cycle can be challenging. However, as a counselor, I can tell you with maximum confidence that there are many practical and effective strategies that can help you manage and reduce fear in your life. And by learning to cope with anxiety, you can prevent it from controlling your life and start living more freely. But before we get into these ways and strategies, I would like us to drum up even more understanding of the concepts of fear and anxiety so we're well familiar with the psychology behind them.

What Causes Fear?

Many things can trigger feelings of fear. Being afraid of certain things (think fires, being robbed at night/being in shady-looking locations, etc.) can actually help keep you safe. However, the specific things that cause fear and how you react to them tend to vary from person to person.

Understanding *what* makes you afraid and *why* is often the first step toward overcoming anxiety. Speaking of anxiety...

What Triggers Anxiety?

Since anxiety is a form of fear, much of what applies to fear also applies to anxiety. The term "anxiety" is typically used to describe a sense of worry or persistent fear, often *without a specific cause*. Anxiety occurs when fear is focused on something in the future or something that might happen, rather than what is happening in the present moment. Health professionals frequently use the term "anxiety" to refer *to ongoing fear*. The feelings associated with both fear and anxiety are quite similar, seeing as how they stem from the same basic emotion.

How do Fear and Anxiety Feel?

When we experience intense fear or anxiety, our minds and bodies react rapidly. Here are some common symptoms you might notice in the event of fear or anxiety:

1. Your heart races, sometimes feeling irregular.

2. You breathe quickly.

3. Your muscles may feel weak.

4. You may start sweating heavily.

5.   You may experience stomach discomfort/loose bowels.

6.   It becomes difficult to focus on anything else except the fear itself.

7.   You may feel dizzy.

8.   You may feel paralyzed or unable to move.

9.   You may lose your appetite, sometimes quite severely.

10.   You may have hot and cold sweats.

11.   Your mouth may feel dry.

12.   Your muscles may become really tense.

These reactions occur because your body is preparing for a potential emergency, redirecting blood to your muscles, increasing blood sugar, and sharpening your focus on the perceived threat.

With fear, your symptoms will dissipate once the fear/causative element of fear is gone. With anxiety, however, these symptoms may persist over time, accompanied by a persistent sense of worry. You may also become quite irritable, struggle with sleep, develop headaches, find it challenging to focus on work or future plans, experience sexual difficulties, and lose self-confidence.

Why Won't My Fear Go Away and Allow Me to Feel & Function Normally Again?

Fear can sometimes be a brief response to encountering something new. However, it can also become a persistent, daily issue, even when you can't identify the exact cause (this is when it morphs into anxiety.) In fact, so many of the clients whom I have helped experienced ongoing anxiety but couldn't pinpoint a specific trigger.

Everyday life is full of potential fear triggers, and it's not always easy to pinpoint why you're scared or assess the actual level of danger. And even when you recognize that your fear is out of proportion, the emotional part of your brain may still continue to send danger signals to your body. This brings us to this – how can we help ourselves combat and cope with fear and anxiety?

Let's explore this.

How Do I Help Myself? Coping with Fear and Anxiety

I have come up with 7 simple strategies/steps to cope with fear and anxiety. As is the case with sadness, coping with anxiety works best when your strategies are simple, straightforward, and *easy to apply on the fly*, allowing you to apply yourself toward instantly offsetting fear and/or anxiety before they can take over your psyche.

Let's look at these strategies:

1) Take a Break

When fear or anxiety takes over, thinking clearly can be very challenging. If possible, take a moment to calm yourself physically. Step away from whatever is distressing you, if you can pinpoint it, and engage in a completely different activity for 15 minutes or so.

Suggestions:

- Go for a walk

- Take a bath

- Make a cup of tea

- Drink a glass of water

- Practice deep breathing

- Watch a funny skit/video

2) Breathe Through Panic

If you notice your heart racing or your palms sweating (or any of the symptoms we listed earlier in the chapter), try not to resist them. Stay put, uncomfortable as it may be, and allow yourself to experience the fear. Place your hand gently on your stomach and focus on slow, deep breaths. The goal is to help your mind become accustomed to handling panic, reducing the fear of the feeling itself.

3) Keep in Mind That Anxiety Isn't Harmful

Anxiety and fear can feel overwhelming, and you may worry that symptoms like a rapid heartbeat signal a serious health issue. These worries can intensify your anxiety and fear. It's important to remember that your body's reaction to fear is normal—in fact, it's meant to protect you from danger. Merely internalizing, I have found, not only completely changes how you view anxiety and fear, but it also has the effect of considerably offsetting them and giving you an element of control over them.

4) Challenge Unhelpful Thoughts that Cause Fear/Anxiety

Challenging unhelpful thoughts can sometimes be beneficial. By asking yourself the right questions, you can reassure yourself that there's nothing to fear.

For example, if the idea of getting stuck in an elevator makes you afraid/anxious every time you have to use one, you could ask yourself:

- "Have I ever heard of anyone getting trapped in an elevator (and no, movies don't count)?"

- "Does the elevator appear to be malfunctioning?"

- "Is there any reason to believe that help would be delayed if I did get stuck?"

You'll find that "no/not at all" will be the standard answer to most, if not all, of these questions. This will signal to your brain that there is no need to be fearful/anxious about the activity or occurrence, and you'll find that any symptoms you have will die down.

5) Avoid Striving for Perfection

Far too many of us face challenges with "must" or "should" thoughts... we (often unwittingly) believe that life should be flawless, that we must always remain calm, and that strong people never face difficulties.

I used to be firmly in this camp, years ago, and I swiftly discovered once I got into counseling that this mindset only exacerbates our fear and anxiety over time. It's important to recognize that *life is inherently imperfect*, and you don't need to constantly criticize yourself. If you make a mistake, it's fine... there's no need to beat yourself up over it. We all make mistakes. "To err is human," as they say. Once you take this stance, you'll suddenly find that you have so much less stuff to worry and fuss over.

6) Visualize a Peaceful Place

If you're really struggling with a persistent feeling of fear whose root/trigger you cannot pinpoint; take a moment to close your eyes and imagine a place where you feel safe and calm.

This could be:

- Walking along a beach, with waves gently lapping at your ankles.

- Cozying up in bed with your pet cat/dog

- Recalling a childhood memory that's happy, or even just outright funny. Allow yourself to wallow in these comforting images. They will instantly help you relax and soothe away your fear.

7) Reward Yourself

Finally, *celebrate your achievements*, *especially* if they come despite your fears.

You could:

- Treat yourself to a massage

- Enjoy a nice meal out

- Buy a new gadget or a small gift that makes you happy

- Watch a movie or show you've been meaning to watch

You'll find that some of these strategies work better for you than others... different strokes for different folks and all. However, I recommend that you try each and every one of them. Feel free to experiment with different combinations of these strategies to find which ones have the greatest effect on dissipating fearor anxiety.

Up next, we explore the surprising upside of negative emotions, further impressing upon us why we shouldn't look to repress these emotions, but rather embrace and deal with them directly.

Chapter 9: The Surprising Upside of Negative Emotions

Admit it—you probably try to escape or avoid negative emotions the moment they arise, or at least as soon as possible, no? This is in no way surprising, though; we're conditioned to do this in one way or another. Experiencing feelings like *stress*, *shame*, *anxiety*, or *guilt* is painful, and for many of us, we've been conditioned from a young age to view these emotions as a sign of weakness. We thus naturally gravitate toward positive emotions (joy, excitement, optimism, confidence, etc.), which not only feel good but are also of benefit to us. But do you know that negative emotions if harnessed right, can be as beneficial as the positive ones, if not more? It took me a long time to figure this out, and when I did, it completely changed my life, as well as the lives of numerous clients whom I helped take up the same perspective.

For years now, I have trained myself to embrace and assess negative emotions instead of avoiding them and shift from negative to positive states to improve my emotional intelligence. I also take a lot of pride in helping my clients do the same. However, you will only be able to make this shift after exploring what these negative emotions are trying to communicate to you. I have realized that while many of my clients seek my help to find relief from intense negative emotions, they initially don't realize that these emotions are, indeed, their allies as opposed to their enemies.

The very experiences that you are troubled by may actually be pushing you to grow, change, take action, or gain understanding. Let's explore some of the more prominent negative emotions that we may struggle with and how they may actually be of benefit to you if you harness them right.

1) Stress

I'll begin by examining **stress** as a beneficial emotion. We're all too often told that stress is the enemy, and in its extreme form, it's true that it's closely linked to numerous physical and psychological issues. However, what many of us don't realize is that moderate stress can actually be beneficial to us.

Stress energizes us to meet challenges that are troubling us head on, and put a stop to the anguish they're putting us through. Stress sparks our creativity, as we try to tackle and solve the challenges that are troubling us for good. Strength is a great character builder as well, strengthening our psychological and biological resilience and making us even more formidable in dealing with challenges and hardships.

Consider the concept of "Post Traumatic Growth." I have witnessed numerous clients emerge so much stronger and with a new perspective on life after grappling with a particularly stressful experience and eventually conquering it. Nearly all of my clients often find that such experiences not only stretch their coping abilities but also lead to positive changes they hadn't imagined before.

2) Anxiety

Anxiety, too, has its benefits. Think about it – without anxious fellows who anticipated potential problems, and are motivated to do something about them, many innovations may never have come to fruition.

I like to preach that anxious people play a priceless role in society, and that civilization would be many decades behind if we didn't have them—for one, they're less likely to engage in risky behaviors because they foresee possible negative outcomes. The person who's learned to live with and harness anxiety is also more likely than not to be valued by friends and acquaintances for his or her considerate nature.

Away from generalizations, a certain level of anxiety provides the necessary alertness to handle important tasks, like giving a presentation, taking an exam, etc. Without this heightened awareness, tasks may be taken too lightly, resulting in subpar performance. Anxiety also encourages us to prepare multiple contingency plans, making us way more equipped to handle setbacks than someone who is overly optimistic and free of anxiety.

3) Depression

It seems crazy to classify **depression** as being beneficial. But it can, indeed, be so in specific circumstances. Research has actually shown that periods of low mood can actually improve cognitive function[ix]. Rumination, or the process of deeply thinking things over, can help us solve problems and even uncover insights that may be easily missed by those in a happier state of mind.

During times when we're very low or depressed, we automatically tend to focus more on details, and we're a lot less likely to overlook important information and details. In fact, I often tell my clients who are dealing with other issues unrelated to depression that if they have a project in mind, seeking advice from a depressed friend may actually be their best bet in helping them identify potential pitfalls that they may have overlooked. What is more, asking for advice will make their depressed friend feel useful, which may have the effect of diminishing their depressive state.

To add to everything that we've said, a low mood or depressive state can actually enhance your ability to express your feelings, as you've likely spent considerable time reflecting on them, leading to greater clarity when you finally open up. This is not to make light of how serious depression can be but merely to show that depression, as in the case of other emotions, can be more nuanced than completely "bad" in all situations. If you're experiencing depression, please seek medical attention.

4) Anger

A long time ago, I came across a quote that has stuck with me ever since – "resentment may corrode your insides and leave everything mushed up and rotten, but anger burns everything clean and leaves a cauterized, sanitary state." I took the quote to mean that anger, when channeled right, brings about way more positives than negatives.

Anger is an emotion that can greatly empower us and serve as a wieldable tool for achieving our goals. Fortunately, in most cases, anger doesn't escalate into aggression, unless we have deeper-lying issues. Instead, it often drives problem-solving and offers valuable insights into significant issues. However, when anger is not expressed, it can turn inward, leading to depression and other health problems. This is why

I always insist to my clients the need to express their anger, albeit always in a healthy way.

I have also found that anger often masks other negative emotions and highlights when your values are being violated. By expressing anger, we are able to set clearer boundaries in our relationships, helping others understand what is acceptable and what isn't. It's important, though, to avoid letting anger become your default communication style. This may indicate a lack of control over your emotions.

5) Guilt

Guilt serves an important purpose as well. It encourages us to correct our mistakes and make amends when we've wronged someone. As a conscientious person, it acts as very key aspect of your moral compass.

Imagine a world where people committed crimes without feeling any guilt—without that internal warning, harmful actions would persist unchecked. Guilt helps ensure that our morals are in balance. However, it's also very important to recognize that guilt can sometimes be unwarranted, lingering unnecessarily in the mind. It is thus very crucial to distinguish between valid and unwarranted guilt.

6) Remorse

Similar to guilt, **remorse** occurs "after the fact" and contributes to our personal growth, making us wiser in similar future situations—even if those situations never arise. At the very least, remorse allows us to offer others sound advice based on our own experiences. Remorse also plays a role in helping us mature, making us more careful and deliberate in important decisions by drawing on past lessons. By asking ourselves, "What can I learn from this?" we are able to turn remorse into a tool for personal growth.

7) Jealousy

When we think about **jealousy**, it's clear that, despite its negative reputation, it can actually be a powerful motivator for self-improvement. Feeling jealous of someone who inspires you can push you to work harder and aim higher. Jealousy is, in fact, a form of admiration that drives people to achieve similar success in areas they value. Even in romantic relationships, a touch of jealousy can signal to your partner that they hold significant importance to you. In some cases, even, a lack of jealousy isn't seen as a sign of trust but rather as a lack of concern altogether.

We could discuss the benefits of negative emotions endlessly—they play a crucial role in making the human experience more complete. Just as we appreciate light more after enduring darkness, positive emotions are often more meaningful when contrasted with negative ones. The key is to keep these emotions within a manageable range, ensuring they don't become chronic or overwhelming. This balance can be achieved by regulating emotions and preventing them from escalating, which the entirety of Part 2 of this book has been dedicated to. In the end, sadness can bring peace; fear can lead to confidence; anger can empower; confusion can clarify; guilt can foster growth; and regret can lead to wisdom. As such, don't you think it's wiser to embrace these emotions that we so often try to resist?

This chapter brings us to the end of Part II. Part III explores cultivating emotional empathy.

Part III: Cultivating Emotional Empathy

Chapter 10: The Empathy Advantage in Relationships

It's common to have differences in opinions with others. It's common to have differences in opinions on politics, religion, or even something trivial like choosing paper or plastic at the supermarket. Disagreeing is perfectly normal, but if you want to build and maintain meaningful relationships, practicing *empathy* is crucial.

So, what exactly is empathy? Unlike sympathy, which involves feeling sorrow for someone else's misfortune, empathy goes a step further and has you connecting with and understanding another person's feelings. Empathy has you putting yourself in someone else's shoes, and doing so with an open mind.

Empathy is vital in all your relationships, be they with family, friends, children, colleagues, neighbors, your favorite barista, etc. But I always say that the most important person to empathize with is your partner. If you can't connect with the person who matters most to you, then how can you connect with anyone else?

Let's get into the empathy advantage, and why empathy is so very important in relationships.

Why Empathy is Vital in Relationships

Here are seven compelling reasons why empathy is vital in relationships, and why it's a virtue very much worth practicing.

1) It Bridges Gaps:

Disagreements between couples often arise because they struggle to understand each other's perspectives. Whether it's a significant issue, such as deciding to have children, or a much smaller matter, like choosing what to have for dinner (or where to have it), stepping into your partner's shoes can really help bridge differences and resolve conflicts that much easier.

2) It Helps You Provide the "Right Attention":

By empathizing with your partner, you'll better understand how to give them *the attention and love they need*. Putting yourself in their shoes allows you to gauge whether you're being overly affectionate (which is not necessarily a good thing) or not spending enough time with them. Whatever your partner is (a driven professional, a stay-at-home parent, a work-from-home partner, etc.), empathy will help you have a better grasp on their life and expectations of you.

3) It Helps Foster Positivity:

Empathy enables you to bring out the best in both yourself and your partner. By understanding their behavior and how they tackle life's challenges, you are able to gain insight into their world, which can only lead to positive changes for both of you.

4) Empathy is Essentially Compassion in Action:

Gaining the capacity to view the world from your partner's perspective naturally fosters compassion. When you connect with them and truly understand the challenges they face daily, you'll gain insight into why they are the way they are. This understanding will not only help you make their life better but also improve your own.

5) Empathy Has You Walk in Their Shoes:

Empathy is about metaphorically walking in someone else's shoes. We'll move away from the figurative a little here, and be a tad more literal – whether you're imagining yourself in your wife's high heels during a stressful meeting at work, or in your husband's muddy work boots after a long day at the quarry/construction site, understanding their experiences can help shed a ton of light on their behavior. If your partner seems grouchy or constantly complains about work, it's because they want you to understand what they're going through. So, instead of letting their words go in one ear and out the other, it helps to put yourself in their position and respond with empathy.

6) Empathy Cultivates Patience:

Empathy naturally cultivates patience in a relationship. Instead of reacting impulsively, or taking things the wrong way, empathy encourages you to respond calmly by considering the situation from your partner's perspective. For example, I have a client who cooks dinner for her partner several times a week. A month ago, she tried a new recipe, and instead of complimenting her effort, her partner said, "Honey, I preferred the fish you made last week." And this is where she really impressed me. Rather than getting upset, she instantly put herself in his shoes and viewed it as only natural to have different tastes and opinions. By empathizing with him and exercising patience (she acknowledged what he said, and promised to make him fish the next time), she was able to avoid an unnecessary argument over something so trivial as a home-cooked dinner.

7) Empathy Drives Self-Improvement:

Empathy also highlights that a relationship isn't just about you—there are always two sides to every situation. When you empathize with your partner, you can understand why they might be frustrated or upset with you. This perspective encourages positive change, as seeing your behavior through their eyes can actually inspire you to work on your flaws and become a better partner.

Simple Yet Practical Ways to Enhance Empathy in Your Relationships

While the reasons that we've outlined above make it seem ever so obvious that empathy ought to be a key part of every relationship, many relationships nevertheless struggle with a lack of empathy. Why is this the case? Factors such as hectic work schedules, a tendency to fall into patterns of conflict, and never having learned how to express empathy all hinder our ability to truly understand one another. Here are some quick-fire ways that you can enhance empathy in your relationship *immediately*.

1) Schedule Uninterrupted Time Together: Set aside time for just the two of you to talk without any distractions. Turn off all electronic devices to signal, "You have my full attention right now."

2) Listen for Underlying Emotions: Pay attention to the emotions behind the stories your partner shares. If these feelings aren't immediately clear, try to put yourself in their position and imagine what they might be feeling. Alternatively, ask directly, "How did you feel when...?" Then, reflect those emotions back to them.

3) Hold Back on Your Own Input: When your goal is to show understanding, refrain from offering your own perspective, advice, or solutions. Even well-intentioned advice and suggestions can shift the focus away from your partner and onto yourself.

4) Check for Understanding: Before wrapping up the conversation, ask, "Do you feel understood by me?" If the answer is yes, celebrate that success. If not, continue the conversation, keep listening to their feelings, and try again. If you find yourselves stuck, consider a few sessions with a couples' counselor for additional support.

Up next, we build on this chapter and explore perspective-taking as a skill to hone to help you walk in others' shoes better.

Chapter 11: Walking in Their Shoes: Perspective-Taking as a Skill & How to Go About Practicing It

We're all familiar with the saying, "Do not judge another person until you've walked a mile in their shoes." This phrase encourages us to pause and consider what life might be like for others, before assuming we know what's best for them.

But why do we need this reminder? Because, although it may sound easy, truly understanding someone else's experience is anything but. This process involves a key element of empathy known as *perspective-taking*.

Understanding Perspective-Taking

So, what is perspective-taking? From an academic/research standpoint, it is defined as the "mental malleability to deliberately take up the perspective of another" (Decety, 2006, p. 144[x]).

These ten words encompass considerable effort. First, we must thoughtfully engage in considering the other person's situation, which requires us to stretch our minds beyond our own viewpoint and embrace someone else's perspective—this is the "mental flexibility" part. Next comes the "intentionality," the conscious decision to take the time and effort to put ourselves in someone else's position. Finally, there's the action of "adopting the perspective" of others, which means actively seeing the situation from their viewpoint and experience, *distinct from our own.*

Kinds of Perspective-Taking

There are various ways through which we can both understand and observe another person's point of view. Each method addresses different factors that influence how we can process and interpret someone else's thoughts:

1) Conceptual Perspective-Taking/Cognitive Perspective-Taking

The first method is known as "conceptual perspective-taking", or "cognitive perspective-taking". This involves exploring and adopting the other person's worldview, cultural influences, and underlying motivations that may be shaping their behavior. By stepping into their thoughts and beliefs, you are able to gain a clearer understanding of their perspective. The aim of this approach is to *access* and *comprehend* the thoughts guiding the person's decisions, both before and during the interaction. When people think about adopting a new perspective, this is typically the type they imagine.

2) Perceptual Perspective-Taking/Visual Perspective-Taking

Perceptual/visual perspective-taking is yet another perspective-taking approach. This takes place when you *physically place yourself* in the position of the other person and *observe their sensory experience*. You take note of what they see – such as whether their view is obstructed – and what they hear, particularly if there are external factors affecting their ability to understand what you're saying. This method is especially useful when working with someone who is sensitive to their surroundings, as it helps you understand any environmental factors that might be disrupting the conversation or negatively impacting the other person.

3) Affective Perspective-Taking/Social Perspective-Taking

The final form of perspective-taking is affective perspective-taking, also known as social perspective-taking. This involves making a concerted effort to connect with and understand the emotions of others. This approach allows you to truly recognize and comprehend another person's feelings. While it can be challenging, especially when intense emotions are involved, it can significantly aid in conflict resolution by helping you identify the emotional drivers behind someone's viewpoint or behavior.

However, this approach requires strong emotional regulation skills. When you take on someone else's emotions, it's important that you remain calm and be able to extricate and distance yourself if needed. Additionally, it's very important that you do not engage with the emotions at the same intensity as the other person but maintain some emotional distance so you can better understand what they are experiencing.

Practicing Perspective-Taking – How to Go About It

Now that we have a comprehensive understanding of what perspective-taking is, we can explore how to practice it, drawing on years of applied psychology research and insights from developmental psychology. If you are interested in a deeper dive into the benefits and science behind perspective-taking, I suggest exploring topics such as the theory of mind[xi], brain regions and their activation[xii], and the neural basis of perspective-taking[xiii].

The best way to start practicing perspective-taking is by learning about it, which we've already done. Following this, you need to incorporate and apply perspective-taking skills in your day-to-day living. Let's explore these, as well as how to go about practicing perspective-taking.

Important Skills for Perspective-Taking

While most of us have developed our own methods for perspective-taking and problem-solving to whatever degree, this ability can be further refined by focusing on key skills that enhance the process of shifting perspectives in social situations. The following outline provides basic considerations and skills to help you improve your perspective-taking, which can be expanded upon for a deeper understanding.

1) Observe

Start with observation, as it's crucial for identifying the factors influencing another person's point of view. If possible, take note of their physical environment and any unique stimuli present. Consider the person's background if you know them well, and pay attention to the language they use when speaking. The more details you gather, the better you can understand the other person's mindset.

2) Imagine

Next, begin to imagine how the observations you've made interact with the person's physical space, and how these might be affecting their emotions. Picture yourself in their position, experiencing the stimuli around them. Consider how their worldview shapes their approach to the topic at hand. The goal is not to critique or judge, but to gain insight into what drives their perspective.

3) Consider

Next, consider how the factors influencing the person and their proposed solution or idea address the situation. By this stage, you can evaluate their position with more empathy and compassion than if you had jumped to conclusions, as you now understand where they're coming from. This doesn't mean you have to agree with their viewpoint, but it certainly provides valuable context.

4) Share

After considering the other person's perspective, you can share your thoughts with them. If you agree with their position, explain what led you to that conclusion. If you disagree or want to suggest changes, acknowledge that you understand why they offered that solution, and then share your own reasons. This approach encourages respectful dialogue, and allows you to continuously refine your perspectives.

Up next, we explore how to teach perspective-taking to children to make them more considerate and empathetic.

Chapter 12: Perspective Taking: How to Teach this Social Skill to Kids

Perspective-taking as a skill is crucial for children because it underpins most communication and interactions, and it completely reshapes how they interact with others, as well as how capable they are of channeling empathy.

In this chapter, I'd like to share some methods that I use to teach perspective-taking to the kids I work with. I've found that this skill requires significant time and repeated practice for a child to fully grasp and apply it. It's not a skill that can be taught just once, but rather something that needs continual reinforcement. By developing perspective-taking skills, children learn to better comprehend others' feelings and thoughts, leading to more effective communication and a better understanding of others' needs.

Here are methods that you can apply directly to teach perspective-taking to your kids.

#1: Social Scripts and In-The-Moment Teaching

I've discovered that perspective-taking is particularly effective when addressed through *immediate* coaching or teaching. For instance, if you notice a child having difficulty understanding someone else's viewpoint, it's a great opportunity to step in, model the behavior, provide scripts, and support them in grasping the concept right then and there.

Some straightforward social scripts that might be useful include:

- "I can see what you mean."

- "I understand where you're coming from."

- "I hear what you're saying."

- "I respectfully disagree because..."

#2: Perspective Taking and Social Problem Solving

Teaching children how to independently resolve problems using *peaceful conflict resolution skills* is a crucial and essential life skill. While it's unrealistic to expect that children will never face issues or conflicts, it's nevertheless important for them to learn how to handle these situations appropriately.

In my groups, I start each year with activities focused on good sportsmanship. Demonstrating positive sportsmanship is a great example of practicing perspective-taking skills. One approach that I have found to be effective is organizing team-based games, where the focus is on *cooperation* rather than *competition* (think relay races where each child's success contributes to the team's overall performance, etc.) Role-playing scenarios, where children practice how to win or lose gracefully, can also help them understand the importance of empathy and respect for others.

Yet another activity that I like involves creating a "Sportsmanship Pledge," where you have the kids come up with their own set of rules for fair play and respect, which they sign and commit to before participating in any games (or other activities, for that matter). Additionally, I like using storytelling or books about sportsmanship to further reinforce these values by allowing children to see examples of both good and bad behavior in a relatable context.

In addition to this, I also use problem-solving scripts to help children manage conflicts, such as teaching them to use I-Statements like: "I feel _____ when you _____. Could you please _____?"

Another useful strategy that I have found to be quite effective is from the book <u>*A Bug and a Wish* by Karen Scheuer</u>[xiv], which involves the script: "It truly bugs me when _____, I wish you would please _____." It works brilliantly because the child is able to express displeasure in an assertive manner without being crass or making the other party feel attacked.

#3: Perspective-Taking Glasses

I enjoy incorporating props into my work with kids because it makes learning fun! For instance, you can use oversized novelty glasses (you can fashion them from cardboard, etc.) and have the kids wear them while they engage in role-playing activities where they try and adopt someone else's perspective. When a kid's turn arrives, they get to wear these "perspective glasses" to help them take the other person's perspective, and so on.

Alternatively, you can have the kids make their own perspective-taking glasses (perhaps even a monocle) using pipe cleaners. Engaging them in this way may have the effect of getting them even more invested in the perspective-taking class.

#4: Optical Illusions

When introducing perspective-taking, I like to use optical illusions, which I have found the kids find fascinating and gets them even more invested in the process. For example, you can draw the letter "M" on a piece of paper and have two people look at it from different angles. One might see it as a

"W," while the other sees it as an "M." This exercise is a great way to start a conversation about perspective-taking.

There are many optical illusions available online. You can print as many of them as you want, and fashion them into simple-to-use cards that the kids can play with. Consider laminating these cards, though, to keep them intact for as long as possible... I'm sure you know that children are not especially the gentlest when playing with things, especially when said things are made of paper.

#5: Perspective-Taking and Bibliotherapy

I'm a big advocate of bibliotherapy, and books are a fantastic way to teach perspective-taking skills to kids. Depending on the children's age and developmental level, starting with the concept of thought can be helpful. For this, I recommend *What is a Thought* by Amy Kahofer & Jack Pransky[xv].

Another great book is *Duck! Rabbit!* by Amy Krouse Rosenthal & Tom Lichtenheld[xvi], inspired by a famous 1892 illustration. *Stand In My Shoes: Kids Learning About Empathy* by Bob Sornson[xvii] is also worth considering. This book allows for engaging activities, such as creating stories about people who might have worn various shoes, and helping kids understand different perspectives. You could even pair these stories with role-play scenarios.

I also love *The Weird Series*[xviii] (including *Weird!*, *Dare!*, and *Tough!*) by Erin Frankel. This unique series addresses bullying from the viewpoints of the bully, the victim, and the bystander. Lastly, *Hey, Little Ant* by Phillip and Hannah Hoose[xix] is a delightful story that encourages kids to think about what they'd do if an ant they were about to squish started talking to them!

#6: The Respectfully Disagree Perspective Taking Games

i) Sound Game

Playing sound games is a fun and effective way to practice respectful disagreement and perspective-taking. You can play various sounds for the kids and then have them discuss what they think they heard. If a kid has difficulty with taking perspective, they might respond along the lines of, "No! You are mistaken! This is what it really is!" If this happens, it presents a great opportunity for on-the-spot coaching. Additionally, I like to pre-teach the art of respectfully disagreeing and promoting good sportsmanship. Consider doing the same with your own kids.

ii) Guessing Games

For a guessing game, place an object in a box and have the kids reach in and feel around to guess what it is without looking. This game encourages them to practice respectful disagreement. If you're teaching remotely or in a hybrid setting, you can place an object very close to your camera lens and have others try to guess what it is.

These perspective-taking teaching methods are awesome for kids because they are simple enough to apply while keeping the kids invested and interested from the word go. I would recommend that you use them all to truly ensure that your kids' perspective-taking abilities are enhanced.

Up next, we explore the subject of empathy backfiring, and how to prevent emotional burnout.

Chapter 13: When Empathy Backfires: Avoiding Emotional Burnout

Like most people I meet and counsel (and like yourself, I'm sure), I am someone who naturally has a great deal of empathy. I can deeply connect with and understand what others are going through, which is a valuable trait that serves me well as a family member, wife, friend, coworker, and overall person. However, I have learned the hard way that when this quality goes unchecked, it can lead to burnout, exhaustion, and eventually resentment.

Over time, I've come to realize that empathy is one of the reasons I (and a good number of my clientele) struggle to ask for help. It creates a gap between our own wants and needs and causes us to unconsciously prioritize the needs of those around us. We're often so focused on ensuring that the people in our lives feel supported and cared for that we overlook the toll it takes on us.

This chapter explores scenarios that may lead to our empathy backfiring, and how to avoid emotional burnout.

Let's get to it.

Too Much of a Good Thing

I like to use workplace examples because we can all relate to them in some capacity:

In the workplace, it's well-known that empathy leads to happier and more productive employees, and that empathetic leaders foster greater loyalty among their teams. With that said, there's a very clear distinction between being an empathetic, compassionate boss and being a boss who is too nice. In fact, a boss who never offers criticism can be more problematic than one who delivers overly harsh feedback.

The manager who is overly nice may fall into the "Ruinous Empathy" trap, a term that was coined by Russ Laraway and Kim Scott, proprietors of Candor Inc[xx]. This occurs when leaders care deeply about their employees on a personal level but seldom challenge them to improve because they do not want to hurt their feelings and perhaps affect the relationship and rapport they have. And while this may seem like it creates a relaxed work environment – which is the ideal that most workplaces aim for – it actually hinders the employee's growth, as well as that of the entire organization. After all, how can one improve without receiving feedback? Being too nice not only harms the employee's development but can also damage the manager's reputation. Overly nice managers may be perceived by others as thin-skinned or ineffective at making tough decisions.

Away from the workplace, the very same principle applies to personal interactions. While empathy often leads to noble, altruistic acts of kindness toward others, unchecked empathy can be risky, especially when helping someone you don't know. As such, it is important that you prioritize safety even as you try to be empathetic. As Delphine Grynberg and Sara Konrath noted in their research study, "The Positive & Negative Psychology of Empathy[xxi]," overly empathetic and emotionally naive acts of rescue have likely led to premature deaths throughout history.

I'll put it this way... adopting a stray dog/cat is one thing, but taking in a stranger, while well-intentioned, is far more difficult to manage.

Confusing Charity for Empathy

Another way that "empathy" can have negative consequences is when it creates a sense of distance or comfort between ourselves and the people we are helping. Research from the University of Manitoba[xxii] found that when we empathize with a disadvantaged community over an extended period, it can reinforce negative stereotypes we hold about them. For instance, if your only interaction with San Fran's Tenderloin neighborhood is through donating to their clean needles clinics, you may start to believe that the entire area is predominantly inhabited by heroin users. This stereotype may lead to unconscious judgment, and cause you to unwittingly distance yourself from the people in that community.

The same University of Manitoba study also looked at charities that, while helping communities, inadvertently strip them of their autonomy. For example, a nonprofit might build clean water wells but fail to teach local residents how to maintain and repair them. When a well breaks down, the nonprofit must step in to fix it. The study suggests that this isn't true empathy, as it maintains a power imbalance between the advantaged and disadvantaged communities.

Another risk is that empathy can lead to paternalistic behavior, where you unwittingly feel superior for offering help. Acts of charity, like donating money or paying for someone's rent, might be motivated by empathy, but without a genuine connection to the recipient, these actions can start to feel like exercises in power for both parties. When a savior complex develops, this can actually diminish empathy over time, in addition to causing burnout.

Giving Too Much of Yourself

On the other hand, being consistently and deeply empathetic can create its own challenges for you, as the empathizer. When we engage in long or frequent empathetic interactions, we can experience what is known as empathy exhaustion or compassion fatigue. This is a natural response that occurs after repeated, high-effort empathetic engagements. Symptoms of empathy exhaustion include impatience, irritability, aggression, reduced concentration, and a sense of detachment from clients or customers. Essentially, we reach our limit for caring.

Although common, empathy exhaustion is very much preventable. From a self-care standpoint, we can take breaks to listen to music, go for a walk, or otherwise detach from the situation. From a business perspective, we, in our places of work, can help prevent empathy exhaustion both in ourselves and in others by fostering supportive environments where everyone feels comfortable asking for help before they reach their breaking point.

Choose Empathy but be Wise Nonetheless

Understanding and knowing when to apply empathy will prove to be very valuable in avoiding an overwhelming empathy meltdown. As we've seen, empathy is a powerful tool as far as building stronger connections with our community, colleagues, and customers goes, but it does have its challenges. It's very important that we use empathy intentionally, and with consideration for our own mental well-being. And as share empathy with others, remember to show empathy toward yourself as well.

This chapter brings us to the end of Part III. Part IV explores communicating with emotional intelligence.

Part IV: Communicating with Emotional Intelligence

Chapter 14: Curing Emotional Tone-Deafness

A few weeks back, Kevin – one of my clients – practiced his pitch with his wife just before leaving for work, where he intended to ask for more time working remotely from home. On the way to the office that morning, he felt even more confident that his boss would see... scratch that, *should* see his point of view. He believed that after explaining how working remotely two days a week would not only improve his family life but also enhance his productivity and engagement, his boss couldn't possibly disagree. It seemed like an obvious win-win.

Unfortunately, it turned out to be anything but. Kevin laid out his case perfectly, explaining how Jack and Olivia – his two kids – were at such busy stages in their lives and how his wife's longer hours due to layoffs at her company were impacting their family. Nonetheless, all his boss had for him was the blankest of stares.

To Kevin's boss, his pitch just came off like he was asking to work less for the same salary. After what Kevin described to me as a "super-long pause likely spent processing what she saw as an absurd request," she finally replied, "More time away from the office just isn't feasible right now. We're too short-staffed." Then, with a wide smile, she added, "But I'm glad you stopped by because I want to discuss the meeting in Cincinnati next week..."

Looking at Kevin's story, in his boss' mind, she believed she was handling the request professionally and with respect. Even though she was denying his request, she didn't see herself as being harsh. In fact, she thought her smile showed she wasn't a mean person. But Kevin, on the other hand, was left wondering if she was completely oblivious, uncaring, or both.

The Two-Toned Conversation

This scenario unfolds in offices, homes, workplaces, coffee shops, cafes, etc., across the country every day—one person is emotionally zigging while the other is zagging. And it helps to ask yourself... when these mismatched conversations happen in my space, which side of the desk am I on?

A lack of empathy doesn't necessarily come from being inherently rude. Even well-meaning, kind people can sometimes struggle with empathy. It's a skill that some of us simply practice more frequently than others.

Recent research by Michael Kraus at the University of California, San Francisco[xxiii], indicates that people with higher levels of education, wealth, and social status often exhibit less empathy because they see themselves as less reliant on others. This misperception often leads them to practice empathy less often, which negatively impacts their emotional intelligence and causes them to lose touch with others.

However, empathy challenges aren't necessarily limited to the educated and wealthy. Not by a long stretch. If most folks on the more median side of education, wealth, and conventional accomplishments were highly empathetic, we'd have a lot fewer two-toned exchanges between workmates on the same level of expertise, family members, romantic partners, close friends on similar rungs, etc. While the study's participants with more education, wealth, and status perceived themselves as less dependent on others, the same could be said for anyone who has a strong sense of independence, which may explain the detachment seen in many successful and not-so-successful individuals—perhaps even in the person you see in the mirror.

If we're being honest, we can all recall times when we've missed the emotional tone of a conversation or the mood in a room, leading to a tone-deaf response. Even I can recall multiple times when I missed the emotional tone in a conversation, despite being primed to read this sort of thing at a high level owing to my years as a counselor.

Here are three simple ways to improve your ability to "hear" emotional tone:

1) Put Yourself in Their Shoes.

This one is the one-size-fits-all approach when it comes to all things concerning emotional intelligence. In Kraus's study, even the wealthiest participants were able to accurately gauge other people's emotions when they were asked to imagine themselves in a lower socioeconomic position. The ability to empathize with others is always within reach. Simply ask yourself, "If I were in their situation, how would I feel?" We won't go into too much detail on this one since we've already explored it in some detail. But always ask yourself this question whenever you're having an exchange with someone, and you believe that they think you do not get them or their point of view at all.

2) Misery Loves Company, so Provide It when Necessary

Matching the emotional tone of others often means *mirroring their feelings*. Sometimes, this involves adopting a somber expression when someone is clearly upset, and other times, it means sharing in their joy with a smile. When people are happy or excited, they want others to share in that excitement. Conversely, when someone is dealing with a painful experience, the last thing they want is for someone overly cheerful bouncing all over the place trying to cheer them up.

You don't have to fake your emotions constantly. But by genuinely focusing on understanding the other person's experience, you'll naturally begin to mirror their emotions. Even a brief acknowledgment of their feelings, like saying, "I know this must be really hard for you" or "That's so exciting!" can make a big difference. However, even as you mirror their emotions, it will help to retain some level of neutral detachment. The last thing you (or even the opposite party) need is getting overly invested in their emotional state and losing your sense of calm and composure. Doing so may actually throw the whole dynamic off and drive you to the very deep end of the emotions that they're feeling, at which point you stop being helpful to them.

3) Just Ask.

Even the most emotionally intelligent people can sometimes be unsure about what someone else is feeling. The solution is simple and often overlooked: just ask. Seriously...that's all you need to do a vast majority of the time. It's easy to overcomplicate emotional intelligence, but sometimes, the best answer is right in front of you, just waiting to be noticed and tapped into. Merely asking questions and listening intently has many a time helped me gain the perspective of others in ways that I would never have if I had opted for a more "complicated" approach.

Chapter 15: Assertiveness 101: Speaking Your Truth with Tact

One afternoon, I received an email from an author I greatly admire, who sent me a copy of their latest book. I was both flattered and excited.

Eager to dive into the book, I quickly wrapped up my tasks and began reading. While I enjoyed it, as a reader, I felt like the story was missing something... some element was needed to properly tie the prose together and truly make it a compelling, helpful read.

I knew I needed to respond to the author, so I provided some general feedback, wished them well, and mentioned that I had additional thoughts on the book. To my surprise, the author responded, expressing interest in hearing my detailed opinion.

To ensure I wasn't being overly critical, I asked a close friend to read the book as well, believing that two perspectives would be better than one (two perspectives are often better than just one, by the way).

The situation was further complicated by the fact that the author is also the editor of a publication that I contribute to every so often. So, I wasn't sure how my honesty would impact our professional relationship, in addition to our personal one.

As I waited for my friend to finish reading, I struggled with how to proceed. I wanted to be truthful, but I didn't want to hurt the author's feelings. Despite my contemplation, I couldn't find an easy solution.

Once my friend finished the book, we had a brief, honest discussion and confirmed that we both felt the same way.

I was now at a crossroads. My conscience urged me to be honest, but I knew that doing so could create a challenging situation, especially with someone I deeply respect and work with.

In the end, I chose to be truthful and hoped that the author would appreciate my honesty.

When faced with situations like these, how do we balance tact with truth?

1) Understand the 'Why'

When making a decision, it's helpful to ask yourself, "Why?" For instance, in this situation, I needed to understand why being truthful was important. Often, you already know the answer, but saying it out loud removes any excuses or rationalizations.

Generic feedback may be encouraging, but it doesn't offer much value. It can temporarily boost your ego and make you feel good, but honest feedback provides the opportunity for growth and improvement, even when it isn't pleasant to hear.

I admire the author and genuinely want to see them succeed. Given their talent, skill, and passion for writing, I knew that only by being honest could I help them enhance their craft. And to stay true to my own conscience, which is one of my most dearly-held virtues, it was essential for me to be forthright with them.

2) Consider the Person

I had a developing relationship with the author who sent me the book. From what I had heard and observed during our interactions, I felt they were a kind and reasonable individual.

I only provided detailed feedback after they specifically asked for it. I suggest that before offering your thoughts, you confirm if the other person genuinely wants to hear them.

Some people claim they want honest feedback, but what they actually seek is only positive reinforcement. In those cases, it's best to be tactful and polite, as they may not be ready or willing to truly listen to your opinion.

Receiving critical feedback can be challenging, especially after putting in a lot of effort. However, when someone is genuinely open to hearing the truth and has the emotional maturity to process it, being truthful is always the better choice.

3) Truth Builds Trust

Telling the truth is often difficult, but avoiding reality or being overly tactful isn't helpful either. When someone asks for your opinion, do understand that they are placing their trust in you to be honest with them. It's important that you honor that trust by being truthful.

Honesty is a key component of building trust in any relationship. While the truth can sometimes be painful and even risk damaging the relationship, trust that, in time, the person will understand why you chose to be honest and will appreciate your candor.

However, being truthful may sometimes mean being prepared to let go of certain relationships. Not everyone is ready to hear the truth, understand the intention behind your feedback, or see things from your perspective. I am pretty sure that you already know this to be true, at least on some level, going by varied interactions you may have had in the past.

Letting go can be challenging, but it's worth remembering that the relationships you do maintain are meaningful because they are built on a strong foundation of trust.

In the popular tale "The Emperor's New Clothes," the child bravely tells the truth, saving the king from further humiliation. This act of honesty was both *courageous* and *helpful*. And while there are dozens of figurative meanings and lessons to be drawn from that particular story, the point still stands that whether you adopt a literal or figurative stance when drawing meaning from it, the elements of courage and genuine helpfulness on the child's part still shine through.

In our daily interactions, we often worry so much about hurting others' feelings that we hold back our true thoughts and opinions. But choosing tact or silence over truth only leads to superficial relationships.

We can respect others' feelings while still being truthful by expressing our thoughts kindly and compassionately. When the intent behind sharing the truth is genuinely helpful, it usually comes across that way.

Before choosing to speak, consider these four questions:

1) Why exactly am I intent on telling the truth?

2) Will I regret my tactfulness?

3) Am I invested in total honesty, even though it may mean losing/ruining the relationship?

4) Is the person I'm about to talk to interested in knowing the truth?

If the answers to all 4 questions are positive, then speak your truth as candidly and with as much respect as possible. All will ultimately be well.

Up next, we explore the subject of conflict resolution.

Chapter 16: The Science of Conflict Resolution

Before we get into the ways and steps for effective conflict resolution, I would like to provide a little preamble for the subject first:

Understanding Conflict Resolution

I describe conflict resolution as the process by which two or more parties find a peaceful solution to their disagreement. This disagreement could be personal, financial, political, or emotional in nature. Regardless of the nature, when conflicts arise, negotiation is often the most effective approach to resolving the issue.

The goals of negotiation are:

i) To create a solution that all parties can agree upon

ii) To work quickly to find this solution

iii) To strengthen, rather than damage, the relationship between the conflicting groups

Conflict resolution through negotiation can (and often does) benefit everyone involved. Typically, each side gains more through negotiation than they would by simply walking away, and it can be a means for your group to access resources that might otherwise be unattainable.

With this covered, how should you go about resolving conflict?

Resolving Conflict: A Step-by-Step Guide

1) Understand the Conflict

Conflicts can arise for various reasons, so it's important to clearly define your own position and interests, as well as understand those of the opposing party. To better grasp the conflict, consider asking yourself the following questions:

Interests

i) What are my interests?

ii) What do I truly care about in this conflict?

iii) What do I want?

iv) What do I need?

v) What are my concerns, hopes, and fears?

Possible Outcomes

What types of agreements could we potentially reach?

Legitimacy

i) Is there a neutral third party who could convince one or both of us that a proposed agreement is fair?

ii) What objective standards might persuade us that the agreement is fair? For example: a law, expert opinion, the market value of the transaction, etc.

iii) Is there a precedent that could support the fairness of the agreement?

Their Interests

i) What are the interests of the opposing side?

ii) If I were in their position, what would I care about most in this conflict?

iii) What do they want?

iv) What do they need?

v) What are their concerns, hopes, and fears?

Understanding the underlying interests is crucial for effectively resolving conflicts. All too often, groups waste time "bargaining over positions" without explaining the interests behind those positions. This approach is unproductive because it forces parties to cling to a narrow stance. Once committed to a specific position, it becomes difficult and embarrassing to back down, leading to more effort spent on "saving face" rather than finding a mutually beneficial resolution. Instead, it's more effective to explore the interests of all parties involved and then identify positions that align with those interests.

2) Communicate Clearly with the Opposite Party

Once you've considered both your interests and those of the other party, it's time to engage in direct communication with them.

Here are some tips for holding productive discussions:

i) Listen Attentively: The other party's opinions matter because they are the source of the conflict. Recognizing their concerns is important, though recognition doesn't mean agreement.

ii) Encourage Participation: Allow everyone who wants to contribute to have a voice. Those who participate are more likely to be invested in finding a resolution and reaching a compromise.

iii) Express Strong Emotions: Share your emotions openly and allow the other side to vent their feelings as well.

iv) Stay Calm During Emotional Outbursts: Instead of reacting negatively, try responding with an apology. Apologizing is a low-cost but very often effective technique.

v) Practice Active Listening: Rephrase what you're hearing as a question to ensure understanding, such as, "Let me see if I understand. You're saying that... Is that correct?" This shows you're listening, even while maintaining your stance.

vi) Speak from Your Perspective: Focus on your own feelings and experiences rather than accusing the other party. For example, say, "I feel upset knowing my children are reading this outdated textbook," instead of, "How could you choose such a biased book?"

vii) Be Specific Yet Flexible: Discuss your interests rather than rigidly sticking to a position.

viii) Avoid Rushing to Judgment: Keep asking questions and gathering information before forming conclusions.

ix) Collaborate on Solutions: Don't place the burden of resolving the conflict solely on the other party. Work together to find a solution that benefits everyone.

x) Make Their Decision Easier: Find a way for the other side to agree with your position without feeling like they are compromising their dignity. While egos are significant in negotiations, avoid framing it as helping them "save face."

3) Brainstorm Potential Resolutions

With a clear understanding of both parties' interests and effective communication strategies in place, you can now focus on generating solutions. Review the interests you identified for both yourself and the opposition, and look for areas where your interests overlap. Often, both sides share common goals (a desire for stability, mutual respect, etc.)

Before holding a brainstorming session, carefully plan how to structure the meeting. Start by drafting a clear purpose statement. Limit the group size to 5-8 participants to keep the discussion manageable. Choose a different, informal setting from your usual environment to help everyone feel comfortable and safe. It's also crucial to have an unbiased facilitator who can guide the meeting without expressing personal opinions on the conflict.

When it comes to brainstorming, decide whether you'll do it with the opposing party or just within your own group. In either case, establish some ground rules:

i) Encourage Creativity: Focus on generating as many ideas as possible without judging or critiquing them initially.

This will help keep the brainstorming process open and creative.

ii) Expand Your Options: Aim to maximize, rather than limit, the possibilities on the table.

iii) Seek Win-Win Solutions: Look for compromises where both sides can achieve something they desire.

iv) Simplify Decision-Making: Make it easy for the other party to agree to a solution.

Also, during the session, arrange seating so that participants are side by side, facing the "problem"—which could be represented by a blank chalkboard or a large pad of paper for noting down ideas. The facilitator should start by reiterating the purpose of the meeting, reviewing the ground rules, and securing everyone's agreement to follow them. Throughout the brainstorming, the facilitator will record all ideas on the board or paper.

4) Choose the Most Suitable Resolution

Once the brainstorming session is over, you'll need to determine which resolution is the most suitable. Review the ideas generated and highlight the strongest ones—these are the options you'll focus on during the conflict resolution process. Schedule a time to discuss and evaluate which idea stands out as the best.

The aim is to leverage the skills and resources of both groups to achieve the best possible outcome for everyone. The resolution that provides the most benefit to both parties is likely the optimal choice.

5) Have a Third-Party Mediator in Place

During the brainstorming and selection of resolutions, you may consider involving a third-party mediator. This individual – who must be neither from your group nor the opposing one – should be someone both sides trust to be impartial. A mediator can aid in establishing a standard for evaluating your resolution, such as expert opinions, legal guidelines, precedents, or widely accepted principles.

The mediator might also facilitate your brainstorming session and take on additional roles, including:

i) Setting ground rules that both parties agree to (e.g., agreeing not to discuss the dispute publicly)

ii) Creating a suitable environment for meetings

iii) Suggesting potential compromises

iv) Acting as a neutral listener to both sides' concerns and emotions

v) Clarifying each side's position to the other

vi) Identifying the underlying interests behind each position

vii) Seeking win-win solutions

viii) Ensuring both parties remain focused, reasonable, and respectful

ix) Preventing any party from feeling they are "losing face"

x) Drafting the agreement between the parties

6) Explore Alternatives

Sometimes, despite your best efforts and intentions, you may not be able to find a satisfactory resolution to the conflict. It's important to anticipate this possibility before starting negotiations. Determine in advance when you might decide to end negotiations and what alternatives you have if an agreement cannot be reached.

Early in the negotiation process, brainstorm possible alternatives to resolution and keep your best alternative in mind. Then, as you consider potential agreements, compare them to your "best" alternative. Without knowing your alternatives, you may be negotiating without complete information, which opens up avenues for new problems and issues to creep in.

In order to develop a proper alternative that truly serves both sides, start by brainstorming various options. Evaluate the advantages and disadvantages of each one, considering which are realistic and practical. Also, think about how you can improve each option.

Additionally, consider the alternatives available to the opposite party. Reflect on why they might choose those options and how you can make your alternative more appealing than theirs.

If you follow all of these steps as outlined, you should have very few issues finding a resolution to conflicts, regardless of their nature or severity. As a matter of fact, I have had such overwhelming success following this particular model that I'm yet to feel pressed at all to add an extra step, or even modify it beyond its present state.

Up next, we explore talking someone down from an emotional ledge.

Chapter 17: Talking Someone Down from an Emotional Ledge

Not too long ago, I was speaking to a well-accomplished client and out of the blue, he said to me "I have this high performing employee who's on a particularly precarious ledge. How do I talk him down from it?" In this chapter, I will discuss exactly what I advised him to do.

But first, a word on "the ledge."

On the Ledge

While we're referring to being on the ledge in a figurative sense, it is, however, crucial to recognize that individuals in genuine psychological distress may need professional help. The advice outlined in this chapter is not intended for those who are contemplating suicide... just someone who's reached an emotional cul-de-sac of sorts and needs some help navigating things. If someone you know (be it a family member, friend, colleague, etc.) appears overwhelmed or unable to manage their situation, it is very important that you be on the alert and recommend a psychologist. If said person is a workmate, contact HR as soon as possible, and if an Employee Assistance Program (EAP) is available, provide them with relevant resources immediately.

With this said, let's now get to the advice I gave to my client.

What Not to Do

Let's begin with what to avoid, as these are often the initial reactions we have!

You might be tempted to dismiss or contradict the person's feelings, especially if they seem irrational to you. For instance, if someone whom you hold in especially high regard and who seems to have their stuff together expresses doubts about their abilities or feels they're not contributing enough, be it in a familial, romantic, professional capacity, etc., you may instinctively respond with, "Are you serious?!? You're amazing!" or "Everyone appreciates you."

While these positive affirmations might be true, they can come across as dismissive and invalidating and are quite unlikely to address the core issue.

[I would urge that you take a pause here and re-read what you've just read.]

It's all too possible to offer praise that, while well-intentioned, dismisses and invalidates the person's feelings.

I often tell my clients (and I made sure to tell this particular one) that when it comes to applying yourself like an emotionally intelligent person, facts matter less than you may think. In this case, it's more significant to the individual how they feel about their performance as a partner, family member, parent, workmate et al, than whether they're actually letting others down. Contradicting their perception may seem like a win, but you've missed the point that their struggle is rooted in their *emotions*, not just the *facts*.

Invalidating their concerns can lead to feelings of embarrassment or discomfort, which may make them reluctant to open up to you again. Don't be surprised if they seek support from others who seem more empathetic.

With this covered, let us now explore what to do.

What to Do

Instead of insisting on your own viewpoint, try joining them where they are... basically, join them on the ledge. If your colleague at work (or even your partner, family member, etc.) expresses frustration by saying, "I'm thinking of quitting my job, I can't handle this anymore," begin by acknowledging their feelings and showing that you take their words seriously. You might say, "It sounds like you're feeling overwhelmed and considering quitting. That's important," or "I appreciate you sharing how you're feeling."

Then, ask if they're open to discussing their situation further. For example, "Would you be open to talking about this?" or "Can I ask you a few questions to see if I can offer some support?" Respect their response—if they agree, continue the conversation; if they decline or hesitate, don't press. Instead, offer, "Your feelings matter to me. Whenever you're ready, I'd like to understand more."

Gently inquire about what's causing their distress. You might ask, "What's happening?" or "Can you tell me more about what you're experiencing?" Use neutral questions unless they've specifically mentioned feeling overwhelmed, in which case you can ask about that. Avoid subjective or judgmental phrasing.

As you listen, try to discern the situation's details—what are the facts, and what are the emotions involved? Identifying the specific emotions can be very useful. If you struggle with differentiating between emotions, consider using an emotion wheel[xxiv] to help clarify.

Share your observations or impressions, such as, "I'm sensing that you're not just tired, but also feeling angry." Understand that your initial perceptions might not always be accurate, and that's okay—feel free to try again. Many people appreciate having someone listen and help them untangle their thoughts. If you're off the mark, they will let you know.

Once you have a clearer understanding of their emotions, assess what their values are and how those values might be challenged by their current situation. For example, are they deeply conscientious and worried about letting others down? Or are they passionate about, say, their workplace's mission, or the goals and dreams they have for their children, and are feeling their efforts aren't making a significant impact?

Then, help them identify their feelings and link these emotions to their core values. You may offer a different perspective, like, "I understand you feel the presentation didn't go well, but I noticed the valuable feedback you received and how engaged everyone was. What positive takeaways can you use from their comments?" If you do this, then by and by, you'll get them off the ledge and into a more positive mind space where they can assess everything from a more hopeful perspective.

Encourage forward-thinking by asking questions such as, "How could you prepare differently next time?" or "What follow-up actions might be needed?" Offer your support by asking, "How can I assist you?"

Once you've shown empathy and understanding, it's appropriate to share your perspective. For instance, "I'm glad you talked to me about how you felt after the presentation. I understand now, and I want you to know that I have complete confidence in you and value your role on the team. Feel free to come to me with any concerns anytime."

If someone you manage is feeling overwhelmed, join them in their emotional space, at least temporarily. Show your support and solidarity, then see if you can work together to come up with a plan that helps them feel more positive and motivated to move forward.

This chapter brings us to the end of Part IV. Part V explores emotional intelligence in relationships and its application.

Part V: Applying EQ in Key Relationships

Chapter 18: Emotional Intelligence for Romantic Partners

Emotional intelligence plays a very crucial role in sustaining long-lasting intimate relationships, primarily because it heightens our awareness of the ongoing changes—both big and small—within both ourselves and our partners. Developing your EQ also enhances your sensitivity, something we all desire in a significant other. And with heightened awareness and empathy, you'll intuitively notice subtle shifts in your relationship's dynamics and all for the better.

I'm a firm believer that we all have the potential to achieve the kind of love that we dream about—profound intimacy, mutual kindness, genuine commitment, and deep caring— thanks to empathy, which we've explored in great depth in this book. However, reaching the pinnacle of romance requires all the elements of a strong EQ: sharp emotional insight to distinguish between fleeting infatuation and enduring love; acceptance to process emotions that could damage a relationship if ignored; and continuous awareness to evaluate what's working and what isn't.

Fortunately, you don't need to have mastered EQ before entering into love. Not at all. In fact, I have found that the couples that best master EQ are those that have had turbulent emotional times before its mastery, perhaps because those issues in the past, after their solution, helped bring them even closer and forge a stronger bond. This is why some of the most passionate lovers are in their eighties— they've gone through it all and have learned a great deal about themselves and each other through the years. And when they nurture their EQ on top of it all, their relationship is all but unbreakable.

With all this said, what are some ways that nurturing and leveraging EQ benefits our romantic relationships?

Benefits of EQ in Romantic Relationships

1) EQ helps us to embrace change in our romantic relationships instead of dreading and rejecting it

EQ helps us confront our fear of change, as it helps us internalize that change is an inevitable element in relationships and life in general. When you confront your fear of change (and we all have this fear), you realize that different doesn't necessarily mean worse—oftentimes, things actually improve after change. I have come to learn to view relationships as living entities that naturally evolve.

Cultivating EQ has led me to learn that without guiding that growth in a direction that we desire, it may shift in a way that we don't want.

Ask yourself: Does my partner need something new from me? Is it time to reassess our relationship together? Are external factors requiring a shift in our roles? Are we as content as we once were? Without EQ, these questions can seem too daunting, leading many couples to ignore signs of change until it's too late. But with EQ, these questions not only come to us naturally, but we're also able to pause and actually respond to them, as opposed to reacting.

2) EQ makes it easier to maintain laughter in our love life

Here's something I preach often: to avoid overthinking emotions, you need acceptance. And laughter is a very key part of that.

Couples who can't laugh together about themselves may struggle to accept their relationship, making it harder to tolerate its unique flaws and inevitable missteps—just as they may struggle to accept their own imperfections. They're also less likely to enjoy the relationship's pleasant surprises. With a high EQ, however, you can keep improving your relationship without being trapped by rigid expectations of perfection, and you will have a way easier time laughing together – or even at yourselves – because you understand that neither you nor your partner are perfect or need to be.

3) EQ makes it possible to accurately assess how you feel when your partner is not around & right the ship if you realize that something's off

You can assess the overall state of your life (and relationship) through three key indicators of well-being:

i) Do you feel restless/irritable, generally?

ii) Do you find yourself struggling to get through the day at work or school, even after enjoying a superb night with your partner?

iii) Do you feel resentful toward family and friends, despite spending every possible moment alone with your partner?

Love doesn't thrive in isolation. If you don't consistently feel energized, clear-headed, and positive *away from your partner*, it doesn't matter how affectionate you are when you're together. If your sex life is great but you're slipping at work, or if you feel secure hearing "Hi, honey" when you come home but struggle to get up in the morning and attack your day, then something's off—even if everything seems perfect when you're with your partner.

And this is where EQ comes into play. When this happens, the insights that you gain from your emotions and intellect about yourself, your partner, and your relationship *through nurturing and leveraging your EQ* will help guide you toward the best remedy for your specific situation.

With this covered, let us now explore ways to "love smart."

10 Ways to "Love Smart"

Whether you're new to love or just beginning to explore emotional intelligence (EQ), following these tips will help you navigate your relationship with greater confidence:

1. **Use the three gauges of well-being that we just outlined to guide your romantic decisions.** If your relationship leaves you feeling energized, mentally clear, and more loving overall, it's a good sign that it has a promising future. If not, something is off, and a solution is needed to keep your relationship healthy. Consider brainstorming with your partner to see what might be wrong.

2. **Express your feelings to your partner.** Communicate your emotions openly, as they define who you are. Pretending to be someone you're not will prevent you from experiencing true love.

3.   **Listen with emotional awareness.** Pay attention to your partner's emotions as you listen to their words. Make sure that you tune in to their feelings, as well as their expressions.

4.   **Provide the support and love your partner needs.** Some people appreciate suggestions or a helping hand, while others may find such actions intrusive. Understand that not everyone enjoys affection in the same way. Find out what kind of support and love your partner finds most ideal and mold your actions accordingly.

5.   **When uncertain, ask.** Love doesn't mean you'll automatically know everything. If you're unsure how your partner feels about something, asking is the only way to find out.

6.   **Be ready to invest in the relationship.** Finding true love or fixing any issues that were present via empathy and nurturing EQ via the methods explored in this book doesn't mean the work is over. Understand that relationships *need* ongoing attention to grow and flourish, or they may *wither* from neglect.

7.   **Learn from your partner.** Staying *actively aware* prevents you from relying on outdated assumptions and

keeps your relationship fresh. Look to constantly learn from your partner on what works for them and what doesn't and then act and love accordingly.

8.   **Beware of emotional memories.** Past hurts can be particularly harmful in current relationships. As such, be mindful of emotional baggage, both in yourself and in your partner. Discuss any potential emotional baggage that you may both have and then work together to find a way forward.

9.   **Admit your mistakes.** The complexity of relationships means that mistakes are inevitable, but growth comes from acknowledging them and moving forward without blame.

10.   **Embrace change as a growth opportunity.** While change can be stressful, it also offers a chance to renew and strengthen your relationship. Embrace change and leverage it to improve your relationship dynamics

Example of How Emotional Intelligence Can Improve Romantic Relationships

Emily and Jake have been together for three years and love each other deeply. But lately, they have been arguing more often. After a series of heated disagreements about how they spend their weekends, Emily decides to approach things differently. Instead of reacting out of frustration, she makes a concerted effort to pause and reflect on her feelings. It is only then that she realizes that her irritation and constant argument stems from feeling disconnected and wanting more quality time with Jake. In fact, when she thinks about it, she can't recall the last time they had some quality time together, which was something she deeply cherished early into their relationship.

So, Emily gently shares her feelings with Jake. She's very careful to use "I" statements to express her emotions without blaming him. She says, "I feel lonely when we don't spend much time together." Jake, who usually feels attacked during arguments, instantly notices the difference in her tone and approach. Instead of becoming defensive, he listens carefully and recognizes that Emily's concern actually comes from a place of love, and that she isn't just being combative for the sake of it, as he's believed for some time.

Chapter 19: Cultivating "True Friendships" via Emotional Intelligence

In today's world, where the term "friend" is all too often linked to shallow connections formed on social media, finding true friendship is becoming increasingly rare. True friends stand by you through thick and thin, offer honest feedback instead of just telling you what you want to hear, and encourage you to become the best version of yourself— qualities that are particularly valuable for entrepreneurs and business owners.

So, rather than just seeking more friends, your goal should be to cultivate "true" friendships. But to have true friends, you must first be a true friend yourself. How can you achieve this? Well, emotional intelligence is key.

I have come up with five basic principles of emotional intelligence that can help you build more meaningful friendships... ones that will benefit both your personal life and your business.

Let's look at them.

Principle #1: The "Milk Carton" Rule

The milk carton rule is anchored on this principle: instead of fixating on what you can't change, *direct your energy toward what you can control.*

The milk carton rule comes from a psychology textbook example, where a husband continually gets frustrated with his wife for forgetting to put the milk back in the fridge, resulting in warm milk for his cereal. The therapist helps the man realize that the solution to preserving the relationship isn't to keep trying to change his wife's behavior but to find alternative solutions to the problem—like buying two cartons of milk.

This approach is valuable because, no matter how strong a friendship (or any relationship) starts, there will come a time when each person's habits begin to annoy the other. The instinctive reaction might be to demand that the other person change. However, most people don't change... at least not on someone else's timeline. By applying the milk carton rule and focusing on what you can control instead of trying to change the other person, you can reduce frustration for both yourself and your friend (or your partner, even), which will help lead to a healthier relationship.

Principle #2: Disagree & Commit

"Disagree and commit" originated as a management principle, but it also serves to enhance emotional intelligence.

The idea is to first promote open discussion and healthy disagreement. However, once a decision is made, even those who disagree must "commit" to it. This means that even if you disagree with the final decision, you nevertheless have to fully support the decision and do your best to make it work.

"Disagree and commit" can strengthen both personal and professional relationships because when you consistently go all in with people you trust, they're a lot likelier to reciprocate.

Principle #3: The Rule of Re-thinking

The rule of rethinking is straightforward: When you encounter information that challenges your beliefs, resist the urge to dismiss it. Instead, make a conscious effort to listen and then use any available evidence to reconsider the new idea.

This rule is valuable as it's easy to become emotionally attached to our beliefs, and none of us enjoy being wrong. However, we all make mistakes at times, and the bigger the issue, the harder it is to accept when we're wrong. By practicing the rule of rethinking, you can keep your emotions in check, which will allow you to benefit from the knowledge and strengths of your friends and people around you.

Principle #4: Help First

The "help first" rule suggests that if you're facing a challenging situation and notice someone else in difficulty, try offering help *before seeking it yourself.*

This may seem counterintuitive. When you're struggling, it's all too natural to think, "I need help right now; focusing on others is the last thing on my mind."

However, by helping others first, you effectively tap into *the power of empathy.* Shifting your attention from your own issues to those of others can quickly create or enhance a connection. As others witness your willingness to assist, they are likely to be moved to support you in return.

Helping first also disrupts the cycle of self-focus and misunderstanding, defying expectations. It not only improves your own sense of well-being but also boosts the mood of those you help. This helps to cultivate relationships that are built on trust and collaboration, both of which are key pillars to successful and long-lasting relationships.

Principle #5: The Chess Player Rule

If you've ever observed chess players in a park or played armchair quarterback on a Sunday, you might have cringed at someone's major mistake, thinking, "Oh dear me, how could they fumble so badly?"

But the reality is, many of us would make similar mistakes if we were in their position—it's far easier to spot potential errors when we're not emotionally involved.

The chess player rule highlights that when you're in a high-pressure situation, your perspective is significantly different from when you're not. This rule is based on a psychological concept called *the perspective gap*, which suggests that we often misjudge how we would react (or have reacted) in intense situations.

Understanding this can help us become more empathetic toward others. Instead of thinking, "It's not a big deal; they just need to toughen up," we can shift to asking, "How can I help?"

This shift *from judgment to support* helps build connections rather than creating distance. It makes a positive emotional impact on the other person and has the effect of strengthening your relationship.

Remember, to have friends, *you need to be a friend*. Apply these five principles of emotional intelligence so you can be a dependable friend that others can rely on. Rest assured that when this registers with them, they will reciprocate.

Example of How Emotional Intelligence Can Forge Stronger Friendships

Sarah and Mia had been best friends since childhood. They usually got along great, but lately, Sarah noticed that Mia seemed distant. Whenever Sarah suggested having a girls' night out, Mia would make excuses or seem uninterested. Naturally, Sarah started feeling hurt. She started to wonder if Mia didn't want to be friends anymore.

But instead of letting these feelings fester, Sarah decided to approach the situation with tact and grace. She reminded herself that there may be more to the story and that it was important to actually listen and understand Mia's perspective. The next time they met up, Sarah gently brought up how she was feeling. "I've noticed we haven't been spending as much time together, and I'm worried something might be bothering you. Is everything okay?"

Mia hesitated at first but then opened up. She explained that she had been going through a tough time at work and was feeling overwhelmed. In fact, the pressure was so intense she was seriously considering quitting. She hadn't wanted to burden Sarah with her problems, so she had been pulling away. Sarah listened without interrupting, and then, as any true friend would do, reassured Mia that she was there for her, no matter what.

Mia felt relieved and grateful that Sarah had noticed her struggles and cared enough to ask. Their conversation helped Mia realize she didn't have to face her challenges alone, and it brought them closer together. By using emotional intelligence, Sarah was able to strengthen their friendship, killing two birds with one stone by turning a

---

Chapter 20: Navigating Family Drama with Emotional Finesse

We all encounter family drama at some point. It may be conflicts with siblings, disapproval from a parent or child regarding a personal decision, or more serious issues like divorce, substance abuse, or family members rejecting parts of our identity.

As a counselor, I have come to learn that a lot of the time, family drama is exacerbated by inherent power dynamics—such as between parents and children or among siblings—or by imbalances created by financial dependence or cultural norms.

Regardless of the causative element in your case, growing up in a family marked by significant drama, dysfunction, or unresolved issues can affect your mental health, self-esteem, and ability to build healthy relationships, among other things.

While each family situation is unique, there are fundamental strategies you can use to manage conflicts, identify dysfunctional behavior, and take care of your own well-being.

Let's explore these.

Tips and Strategies to Help You Resolve Family Conflicts

In some families, issues may be resolved through open and honest communication. However, in toxic or dysfunctional families, resolving conflicts may seem impossible. If you're dealing with an unhealthy family dynamic, there are strategies you and your family members can use to break existing patterns of conflict and find a path forward:

#1: Reframe the Argument

One approach that I have found to be really effective for resolving family conflict is to reframe the issue so that multiple perspectives can be expressed and understood. While it's natural for everyone to want their viewpoint acknowledged, this can sometimes shift the focus to winning the argument rather than finding a resolution. Instead of seeing the argument as you against your family, consider it as you and your family working together against the problem. Viewing it this way may help reduce tension and make it easier to reach fair compromises.

For instance, if you and your child are arguing about his/her curfew, viewing the problem as "my son/daughter has no respect for my rules" may prevent you from understanding their perspective. However, if you see it as you and your child (who enjoys being out at night just as every other young man/woman does) working together to address the issue of staying out too late, you may better grasp their viewpoint and collaborate on a solution.

#2: Be Honest

You may feel hesitant to fully express yourself during a conflict. This could be due to being taught not to show your feelings, wanting to protect others' feelings, or hoping that remaining quiet will resolve the issue faster. However, not being honest about your feelings—something that requires time and self-awareness—can lead to more conflict later. When sharing your feelings honestly, it's important to stay calm and respectful and focus on the specific issue at hand. This will make it easier to communicate your truth with little risk of the other person feeling attacked and the whole conversation/exchange devolving into chaos and conflict.

#3: Stay on Track

In my many years of counseling individuals and families alike, I have found that in families with many unresolved issues, a single argument can sometimes trigger old emotions that have been suppressed.

For instance, if you're arguing about a family member's spending habits because they bought something they couldn't afford, it's important that you *focus on the specific issue at hand*. Understanding others' perspectives and sticking to the current topic of conflict can prevent the discussion from expanding into other areas of your relationship. In the example we just provided, this means *addressing the impact of that particular purchase* rather than revisiting every instance where their financial decisions differed from yours (which is an approach I have unfortunately observed all too often when mediating family conflicts).

#4: Take Breaks and Take Turns

To manage heated discussions, consider allocating specific time slots for each person to speak (for example, five minutes each) and alternate turns within that timeframe. Using a timer can help keep the conversation *structured* and *fair*.

When it is someone's turn to speak, everybody else should listen quietly (this can be quite challenging when emotions are high.) If you find yourself focusing more on how to respond rather than understanding the other person's point of view, take a moment to breathe and refocus on the main issue.

Lastly, if a discussion or argument seems to have veered off-topic or if participants are too upset to engage calmly, it might be best to take a break and return to the conversation later.

#5: Set & Maintain Boundaries

One of the more essential aspects of resolving conflicts (if not *the* most essential) is setting boundaries—limits that you establish to protect and respect your *time, energy, emotions,* and *resources.*

This can look like this:

- If a family member comments on your appearance: "I'm uncomfortable when you make remarks about my looks. If you continue to do so, I'll have to take time away from you."

- If your brother/sister all too often takes your belongings without asking you first: "I feel really disrespected every time you take my stuff without checking in with me first. I'm willing to share from time to time, but I'd prefer you ask first."

- If there's an upcoming holiday involving family members whom you find crass or hurtful: "I understand you want me to come to Thanksgiving, but I often find that some family members are unkind at these gatherings. I can attend briefly but won't be able to stay long," or

"Thank you for the invitation, but I'll pass this time and visit another day."

Once you set a boundary, it's very crucial that you stick to it. Otherwise, it ceases to be a boundary. This may involve reminding others of your boundary if they *forget*, *question*, or *downplay* it. If your needs and boundaries continue to be disregarded, you may need to remove yourself from the situation and reflect on the best way to communicate and address your needs.

#6: Involve a Trusted Third Party

Maintaining objectivity in family disputes can be challenging – even with the steadfast application of the strategies we've outlined above – as each family member contributes their own perspective, past experiences, and unresolved issues. If you've tried the conflict resolution strategies we've outlined here, but find that discussions remain unproductive, become one-sided, or escalate into harmful or dangerous behavior, it may be helpful to involve someone else to mediate the conflict.

This mediator could be another family member, a family friend, or even a therapist who specializes in family dynamics. Regardless of whom you choose to mediate, understand that engaging a neutral third party can offer an impartial perspective and help prevent the conversation from going off the rails, and the whole conflict dynamic resetting back to square one.

Up next, we explore EQ essentials for leaders and managers.

Chapter 21: EQ Essentials for Leaders and Managers

When you envision an "ideal leader," what do you see?

Perhaps, you envision someone who remains calm and composed, regardless of the challenges in their way. Or, perhaps, someone who earns the full trust of their team, listens attentively, communicates openly, and consistently makes well-thought-out decisions.

All of these traits have one thing in common – they reflect a person with *strong emotional intelligence*. In this chapter, we'll explore the EQ essentials for leaders and managers, as well as how you can develop them.

Let's get started.

Essential #1: Self-Awareness

Being self-aware means that you are always conscious of your emotions and that you understand how your feelings and actions *impact those around you*. In a leadership role, self-awareness also involves having a clear understanding of your *strengths and weaknesses* and approaching your role with genuine humility.

Here are a couple of strategies to help enhance your self-awareness:

i) Keep a journal: Keeping a journal and making daily entries can boost your self-awareness considerably. Even spending just a few minutes each day reflecting on your thoughts and tallying them in your journal will really elevate your self-awareness, especially over the long term.

ii) Slow down: This is often one of my top recommendations to my clients. When you experience intense emotions like anger, take a moment to *pause* and *consider why you're feeling that way*. Also, do keep in mind that regardless of the situation, you always have control over how you respond.

Essential #2: Self-Regulation

Leaders who excel at self-regulation are those leaders who are able to consistently maintain control over their emotions, regardless of how daunting or triggering the situation they're dealing with is. They avoid lashing out verbally, making hasty decisions, stereotyping others, compromising their values, etc.

Here are some strategies to help strengthen your self-regulation:

i) Know your values: It is important to have a clear understanding of your core values and what you won't compromise on, and constantly reflect on your own personal "code of ethics." This way, when you're faced with a moral or ethical dilemma, your deep familiarity with your core values will help you make the right decision without hesitation most of the time.

ii) Hold yourself accountable: If you have a habit of blaming others when things go wrong, you need to stop ASAP. It is important that from now on, you commit to acknowledging your mistakes and facing the consequences, unpleasant as the experience may be. This will help you earn the respect of those around you, not to mention you'll be more at peace with yourself and not have your conscience digging at you.

iii) Practice calmness: When faced with situations that you find challenging or stressful, pay very close attention to how you react. If you find yourself venting your stress on others, you can try deep-breathing exercises[xxv] to calm down. Another technique that I have found to be just as effective is to write down your negative thoughts and emotions, read through your list several times, and then promptly tear up the paper and discard it. Expressing your thoughts and emotions on paper is far better than voicing them to your team, seeing as the latter may spark needless conflict, and it will help ensure that your responses are well-thought-out and fair.

Essential #3: Motivation

Motivated/self-driven leaders *consistently work toward their goals* and *maintain exceptionally high standards* for the quality of their work.

Here are some tips to help boost and maintain your motivation:

i) Reflect on why you're in your current role: It's easy to lose sight of what you truly enjoy about your career, especially if you've been at it for years. This is why you need to take a moment, every so often, to remind yourself why you chose your career. If you're feeling dissatisfied and struggling to recall your initial motivation, try using the Five Whys technique[xxvi] to uncover the root of the issue. Addressing the root cause can help you see your situation from a new perspective, and thus help shed more light on it. Additionally, ensure that your goals are both *clear* and *inspiring* so that your motivation levels are always high.

ii) Stay optimistic and find the silver lining: Motivated leaders tend to remain positive, regardless of the challenges they face. Developing this mindset will certainly require practice, but it's a very valuable and worthwhile habit to cultivate. Whenever you encounter a challenge or setback, try to identify at least one positive aspect of the situation. It could be something small (making a new connection or striking a new friendship) or something more impactful (gaining a valuable lesson or discovering that you need to make a drastic change). I have come to learn that there's almost always something positive, provided you take the time to look for it.

Essential #4: Empathy

We've already explored empathy in great detail.

As a leader, empathy is a crucial trait to have, if you are to effectively manage your team or organization. Empathy allows you to both understand and share the feelings of others, which puts you in a better position to support the growth of your team members, challenge unfair behavior, provide constructive feedback, and listen to those in need.

Here are some tips to raise your empathy levels *as a leader*:

i) Closely observe your subordinates' body language: Body language—be it crossing your arms, shifting your feet, or biting your lip—can convey your true feelings about a situation...and it may not be a positive message. Understanding body language is often a valuable skill, especially for leaders. This is because those under you may not be bold enough to tell you how they really feel since you have authority over them. As such, making a habit of reading and interpreting body language is necessary, as it will help you accurately gauge how those under you really feel, even when they don't say it outright. It will also help you to respond appropriately.

ii) Acknowledge emotions: If you ask your assistant to work late again, and you notice disappointment in their voice, acknowledge and respond to their feelings promptly. Express your appreciation for their willingness to put in extra hours and share your own frustration about the situation. If possible, suggest a compensation package for them (perhaps offering time off on Monday mornings, letting them off early on Fridays, etc.)

Example of how Practicing Emotional Intelligence Makes for Better Leadership and more Motivated Employees:

Maria, a team leader at a marketing firm on the rise, noticed that one of her employees, Jake, had been quieter than usual and seemed less engaged in meetings. Instead of ignoring the change and letting the whole thing ride out (employees, after all, often have low ebbs that they eventually get over on their own), Maria decided to approach him privately. She'd prepared and memorized a few open-ended questions for Jake, which she pitched to him after a bit of cheery small talk. Then, she listened attentively as he confided in her that he'd just had his pet dog of 16 years put down, as she'd grown too old and was suffering. He was finding it hard to cope, and it was affecting his work.

By asking after Jake and offering her support, Maria made Jake feel valued and understood. She worked with him to adjust his workload temporarily and checked in regularly to see how he was managing. This approach not only helped Jake feel more comfortable and supported, but it also strengthened his trust in Maria as a leader. As a result, Jake's engagement improved, and even when a rival marketing firm offered him several incentives to move to them, he turned them down, as he deeply trusted and appreciated Maria and wanted to keep working for her.

Part VI: Expanding Your Emotional Range

Chapter 22: Building Emotional Resilience

When things go wrong, how do you respond? Do you tend to recover quickly, or do you come undone?

I like to define resilience as the *inner strength that helps us bounce back from setbacks or challenges*. These setbacks could involve losing your job, facing a particularly grueling illness, dealing with a disaster, coping with the death of a loved one, etc. Without resilience, you might find yourself stuck on problems for far too long, perennially feeling like a victim, or even turning to unhealthy coping mechanisms like substance abuse, eating disorders, or other risky behaviors.

While resilience won't make your problems disappear, it will for sure help you navigate through them, find enjoyment in life, and manage stress more effectively... among other things.

If you feel you're not as resilient as you'd like to be, there are proven exercises to help enhance your resilience. We'll explore these in a bit. But first, let us build on the description I just outlined by exploring the traits of emotional resilience.

The 6 Traits of Emotional Resilience

Emotional resilience encompasses six key elements:

1) Strong Social Support: It has been my observation that nearly all my emotionally resilient clients have a reliable network of support from close friends, family, and loved ones. This network remains steadfast during both calm and challenging times, setting the "resilience tone" for these clients.

2) A Robust Sense of Self: When you have high emotional resilience, you are secure in your identity and purpose. You more than likely possess self-esteem, self-awareness, self-regulation, self-confidence, and emotional intelligence, which helps you stay grounded and make confident decisions way more often than not.

3) Optimism About Improvement: When you have high emotional resilience, you always hold the belief that things will improve, regardless of how grim the situation is. You are assured in your ability to overcome stress and return to a happier, more comfortable state even when the going is so tough you feel like you're on the verge of breaking.

4) Flexibility: Emotional resilience involves the ability to adapt plans as needed. Flexibility helps us handle changing circumstances and manage stress without becoming overwhelmed or, just as bad, losing hope and going off the rails when situations don't go as planned.

5) Healthy Coping Strategies: Effective stress management is vital during tough times. When we're resilient, we adapt to using constructive and positive coping mechanisms to address our feelings and recover from traumatic events rather than adapting to destructive tendencies and spiraling.

6) Calmness Under Stress: High emotional resilience enables us to stay composed during stressful situations. We are better able to regulate our emotions, manage stress effectively, and respond in a calm, measured way, even if we're still very much experiencing distress.

With these traits covered, let us now explore some practical exercises to help you enhance your emotional resilience.

Exercises for Emotional Resilience

A quick word before we get into the exercises for emotional resilience:

To build emotional resilience and well-being, you must train yourself to focus on the aspects of life you can control. If you can't control something, it's best to just let it be and hope it works out for the best... fretting over things you cannot control only makes you anxious and chips away at your emotional resilience.

Two, I like to emphasize the sheer importance of *grounding yourself in the present moment,* even if it may seem minimal. If you're a parent and often struggle to balance family, work, and personal time, prioritizing mental health is absolutely crucial, and you effectively do so via self-care activities[xxvii]. Note that self-care should be intentional and planned, even if it's just a few minutes each day, and it's important to demonstrate this practice to your children.

With this out of the way, let us now explore exercises for emotional resilience:

1) Manage Anxiety with Paced Breathing:

I recommend to my clients that they take a minute each day (just one minute!) to focus on their breath. I advocate for "paced breathing" during this minute, which basically means taking in slow, deliberate breaths.

Here's how to practice it:

i) Inhale deeply and slowly through your nose, filling your lungs completely.

ii) Exhale just as slowly through your mouth, emptying your lungs fully.

Deep breathing not only helps to manage stress and anxiety in the moment, but it also calms your body and signals to your brain that you're prepared to handle what's coming.

2) Resist "thinking traps"

Reflecting deeply on our own thought processes is crucial during uncertain times, and developing this skill will prove quite beneficial in many other aspects of your life as well. As you reflect on your thought process, keep an eye out for "thinking traps," such as:

i) Black-and-white thinking: Viewing situations as either entirely good or entirely bad, with no in-between.

ii) Catastrophic thinking: Always anticipating the worst possible outcome and believing you won't manage if it happens.

iii) Predicting the future: Assuming you know exactly what will happen far down the line. For instance: "I won't be able to return to school, I'll never get the education I've always wanted, and I'll never be able to attend college."

To avoid these traps:

i) Recognize the pattern: Pay attention when you start spiraling into negative thinking. Several cues that may alert you that you're on the verge of these thinking traps include feeling sad, anxious, or hopeless all of a sudden.

ii) Adopt a realistic perspective: Challenge your thoughts by questioning their validity. Talk to a trusted friend or family member to explore what aspects of your thoughts are realistic and identify any possible "gray areas" or more realistic alternatives.

iii) Use a coping mantra: Develop a reassuring phrase to counteract your worries. For example, say, "I'm doing my best, and everything will be OK."

3) Have a gratitude journal

This one, I have found, works for just about everybody. Even young children can benefit from having a gratitude journal. Jot down 3 things that you enjoyed or felt thankful for every passing day in a notebook or journal. These can be simple pleasures (enjoying a snack, spending time with a pet, or making a new acquaintance/friend, etc.) or more profound (your family, friend, home, job, etc.).

When you focus on a "silver lining" each day, it drastically changes your perspective. This change in perspective can positively impact our emotions and how we respond to various situations, which will help us become more emotionally resilient in the long run.

4) Engage in "behavioral activation"

Engaging in "behavioral activation" can go a long way in uplifting our mood and making us emotionally resilient as a result. This concept involves participating in activities that *offer a sense of control and action*. Here are some examples of activation that you can try:

i) Physical: Activities such as exercise, paced breathing, dancing, etc., are beneficial.

ii) Thoughts and Feelings: Engaging in creative activities like drawing, painting, or completing jigsaw puzzles can be helpful. Additionally, participating in outward-focused activities, such as volunteer work, can also be effective.

iii) Mastery: Learning a new skill, such as playing the guitar/piano or using a language-learning app, can provide a sense of empowerment, which will have a positive effect on your mood and emotional regulation.

iv) Sensory: Create a self-soothe kit to manage anxiety by including items that stimulate each of your five senses—something visually pleasing, a pleasant scent, and objects to touch, hear, and taste.

Wrapping up, I understand that when we experience sadness or intense emotions, there is often a tendency to isolate or avoid situations. However, I have found it to be more beneficial to take the opposite approach—engaging with people and getting involved in different activities. For instance, if you're anxious or worried about something, resist the urge to isolate yourself and brood over it and instead go out and meet with a friend or indulge in an activity. You'll find that over time, you're less and less overwhelmed by things and develop an increasingly optimistic stance toward challenges.

Up next, we explore the subject of vulnerability.

Chapter 23: Vulnerability: The Surprising Key to Emotional Strength

As a psychologist, I often get questions about emotional vulnerability. They include:

- What exactly is emotional vulnerability?

- Is it really positive?

- Should I make an effort to be more emotionally vulnerable?

- What would that even entail?

Like many topics I discuss, emotional vulnerability is often misunderstood because it's used in a broad, unclear way. In this chapter, I aim to provide a straightforward, practical explanation of my perspective on emotional vulnerability and how it can be beneficial in your life.

Let's get to it.

Understanding Emotional Vulnerability

For me, the greatest aspect of being human is *our ability to connect with others*. We're naturally wired for it. We live in communities, make families, work in teams, love in partnerships, flourish through friendships, etc. The urge to connect exists in all of us, whether we realize it or not.

However, lately, we're witnessing a rise in loneliness, depression, fractured relationships, and disconnection. What's causing this? The answer is *an increasing alienation of vulnerability*.

Let's unpack this.

Vulnerability *lies at the heart of connection*. It requires a unique blend of *courage, tenderness*, and a *willingness to open up* and be vulnerable. Without vulnerability, true connection is impossible. But society has mislabeled vulnerability as a weakness.

In an effort to protect ourselves, we've become 'strong,' toughening up and shielding ourselves from any potential pain. Unfortunately, by closing ourselves off to vulnerability, we not only guard against hurt but also block out *love, intimacy*, and *connection*. These emotions all come through the same door, *and when we shut it for one, we close it for all*.

Without vulnerability, relationships suffer. Vulnerability says, "Here I am, with all my flaws, fears, secrets, and affections. Please handle with care—these are precious." In return, it invites a response like, "I see you, and it's okay.

You're safe with me. And here's who I am." This exchange fosters closeness, trust, and a sense of belonging... all essential components for healthy relationships.

Vulnerability also means being open to new experiences, people, and the unknown. And as scary as it can be, it is always, always brave.

I know that we often get hurt – sometimes deeply hurt – in our varied relationships. Pain in relationships is an inevitable part of being human, and when it strikes, it can sometimes feel overwhelming. I understand this. However, we can choose how to perceive this pain—we could choose to view it as a sign of a mismatch between parties, a call for redirection, a lesson, etc. Alternatively, we could choose to see it as a warning and decide to shield ourselves from future hurt by avoiding vulnerability. When we make this latter choice, we close ourselves off, and by closing ourselves off to the risks of being vulnerable, we also close ourselves off to the possibilities—the opportunity for joy, intimacy, closeness, gratitude, connection, etc.

Connected or Not: What Makes the Difference?

Brené Brown, PhD[xxviii], a research professor at the University of Houston and an expert on vulnerability, has studied what distinguishes those with a strong sense of connection and belonging from those without. Her research reveals that the key difference is belief—those who feel a strong sense of love and belonging believe they are deserving of it. People who see themselves as worthy of connection tend to experience deeper connections.

When we believe that we are worthy of connection, we are more inclined to reach out to others. We might be the first to say "I love you" or express "I miss you" not just when apart but even as we sense distance growing in a relationship. We are more likely to ask for help and remain open to receiving love and influence from others. We also tend to approach relationships with gratitude and a strong sense of connectedness.

This doesn't guarantee that we'll always get what we want, but it does mean that we are more willing to be open and vulnerable in relationships because we feel less threatened by the potential for shame. If a connection doesn't meet our expectations—if an "I love you" goes unreturned or a request for help is declined—we are less likely to internalize this as a reflection of our own unworthiness. When we are like this, others automatically want to be around us. We are able to give to relationships and receive in return with openness, honesty, abundance, love, and gratitude. Better yet, we are able to embrace vulnerability in the face of uncertainty and create a safe space for those in our lives to do the same.

Daring to Connect: Steps to Embrace and Harness Vulnerability for Greater Emotional Strength and Better Relationships

1) Live with Heart: Follow your true desires by listening to the inner voice that comes from your intuition, experience, and unspoken feelings. This voice guides us to love openly and honestly, to accept love with gratitude, and to walk away when it's no longer there. Move toward what you truly want, even if it means embracing vulnerability—it's the bravest thing you can do. When you live with heart, you'll be able to recognize when something is missing and make the necessary brave steps to fix that hole.

2) Live with Courage: Think of what you would do if you weren't held back by fear of shame. Would you switch careers, pursue your passion, express love, reach out to someone you miss, initiate intimacy, demand more for yourself, end harmful relationships, or fight harder for the one you're in? While you can't guarantee there won't be rejection or disappointment, you can trust in your ability to handle it if it happens—and handle it, you will! There's nothing worse than hovering on the edge of something

meaningful, wanting more but never lowering your guard enough—never being vulnerable enough—to truly let it in.

3) Explore a New 'What If': Challenge your beliefs. Sometimes, long-held beliefs settle in and remain unexamined. Consider whether they still serve you. What might happen if you opened up, took a risk, and allowed yourself to be vulnerable? Often, our actions are driven by a need to avoid shame—a need to avoid any evidence that we're unworthy of love, connection, and receiving what we desire. The more you believe that you're unworthy, the more you'll behave as if it's true, and this will only lead to disconnection. But what if you believed that you were worthy of connection? The risk of rejection is always present... but it's in no way a reflection of any unworthiness within you. Have this in mind at all times.

4) Embrace Vulnerability: According to Brené Brown, those who feel deeply loved and connected understand that vulnerability is essential. They recognize that their vulnerabilities are part of what makes them beautiful—and they're absolutely right. Vulnerability is crucial for forming connections because it involves the courage to be open with another person. It's about expressing the thoughts and feelings that are pressing from within, allowing someone to get closer, letting them in, and sharing without expectations

or hidden agendas. It also means being open to receiving with a genuine heart.

5) *Quick now. Do nothing*: We live in a world that is increasingly focused on the quickest fixes possible. We have little patience for uncertainty or discomfort and often rush to find solutions. We're quick to fix everything—problems, health issues, emotions, even people. However, sometimes, the moments and environments fostered by uncertainty and discomfort are exactly where we need to be. These moments can bring insight and clarity and help us decide whether to move forward or pull back. So, don't be too eager to escape uncomfortable feelings. Oftentimes, they provide the richest opportunities for growth, as well as understanding what is truly right.

With everything that we've covered thus far, I would be remiss not to offer some direction on what vulnerability *isn't*. Let's briefly look at this as we wrap up...

What Vulnerability Is Not

Vulnerability doesn't mean sharing every detail of your life with anyone who will listen. Vulnerability involves great intentionality at its core. There are people in your life—those you hold close or want to get closer to—who are worth the risk of opening up to. You share parts of yourself with these people and hope it will be received positively.

However, not everyone you know deserves that level of vulnerability. As such, your openness *should be earned to some extent,* and you need to be very discerning about who merits it. Revealing every personal detail to a stranger, like the guy behind you in the grocery store checkout line, or even to someone you know but not too well, like a distant cousin or the auntie you talk to a couple of times a year at best can lead to a lack of boundaries and make you feel overly exposed.

Part VII: Lifelong Emotional Growth and Support

Chapter 24: Assessing Your Emotional Intelligence Progress

This book has explored almost every aspect, element, and component needed to truly level up your emotional intelligence levels. If you apply everything we've outlined thus far, you will notice a significant uptick in how you process and regulate your emotions and how you assess and respond to those of others within a very short time.

Nevertheless, the only sure way to know you're making headway is to assess the progress you've made.

I have come up with 7 simple steps to help you with this.

Note: I would recommend that you give it at least two weeks after beginning to apply the lessons in this book before carrying out this self-assessment:

Step 1: Reflect on Your Emotional Awareness

Start by reflecting on your growing ability to recognize and understand your emotions as they arise. Consider recent situations where you've experienced strong emotions—both positive and negative.

Ask yourself:

i) How quickly am I able to identify my emotions? Reflect on whether you are having an easier time labeling your feelings accurately (e.g., anger, frustration, excitement, contentment) or if they often feel vague or overwhelming.

ii) Is there progress in understanding the triggers behind my emotions? Analyze whether you are having an easier time tracing your feelings back to specific events or thoughts and if you can discern patterns in your emotional responses.

Tip: Keep a journal to document your emotional experiences and review it periodically. This practice will help you identify recurring themes and gauge your emotional awareness over time.

Step 2: Evaluate Your Emotional Regulation

Next, assess how effectively you're able to manage your emotions in various situations. Think about recent experiences where you felt stressed, angry, or anxious.

Consider:

i) How well am I able to maintain composure under stress? Evaluate whether you are steadily staying calm and collected in challenging situations or if you still tend to react impulsively or lose control.

ii) Am I now able to "soothe myself" when distressed?
Reflect on the approaches you've incorporated to calm yourself (e.g., deep breathing, taking a walk, or talking to someone) and how effective they are in helping you regain balance.

Tip: Practice mindfulness or other relaxation techniques regularly, and note how they impact your ability to regulate your emotions over time.

Step 3: Assess Your Empathy Levels

Consider how well you now understand and respond to the emotions of others. Empathy is a key component of emotional intelligence, and your ability to connect with others on an emotional level can significantly impact your relationships.

Reflect on:

i) How attuned am I to others' feelings? Think about how often you notice subtle emotional cues in others as of late, such as changes in tone, body language, or facial expressions.

ii) Do I respond compassionately to others' emotions? Assess whether you've made progress in taking others' feelings into account when interacting with them and if you can offer support or comfort when needed.

Tip: Practice active listening and ask open-ended questions in conversations to deepen your understanding of others' emotions. Regularly seek feedback from trusted friends or colleagues to gain insights into how empathetic you appear to others.

Step 4: Review Your Social Skills

Examine how your emotional intelligence translates into your social interactions as of late. Social skills reflect your ability to navigate relationships, communicate effectively, and collaborate with others.

Consider:

i) How well do I manage conflicts? Reflect on how you now handle disagreements or misunderstandings. Have you adapted to approaching conflicts with a problem solving mindset, or do you still tend to avoid them?

ii) Am I now able to influence and inspire others? Think about how your ability to lead or motivate others has evolved recently, whether in a professional setting or personal relationships.

Tip: Engage in group activities or team projects where you can observe and refine your social skills. Pay attention to how others respond to your communication style and make adjustments as necessary.

Step 5: Monitor Your Motivation

Finally, assess your internal drive and how it influences your emotional intelligence. Motivation in this context refers to your willingness to pursue goals, face challenges, and maintain a positive outlook.

Reflect on:

i) Have I grown more committed to personal growth? Consider whether you've made a habit of consistently setting and pursuing goals that challenge you emotionally and intellectually.

ii) Can I maintain a positive attitude even in adversity? Evaluate how well you now stay optimistic and resilient in the face of setbacks.

Tip: Set specific, measurable goals related to your emotional intelligence development, such as improving your response to stress or deepening your empathy. Regularly review your progress and celebrate small victories to stay motivated.

Step 6: Seek External Feedback

To gain a more objective understanding of your emotional intelligence, seek feedback from others who know you well. Ask them to share their observations on your emotional responses, empathy, and social interactions.

Consider:

i) *How do others now perceive my emotional intelligence?* Gather insights on handling emotions, relating to others, and managing relationships.

ii) *What areas do others think I can improve?* Be open to constructive criticism and use it as a guide for further development.

Tip: Consider using a formal emotional intelligence assessment tool, such as the EQ-i 2.0[xxix], to comprehensively understand your strengths and areas for improvement.

Step 7: Reflect and Adjust

After gathering insights from self-reflection, feedback, and possibly formal assessments, take time to reflect on your progress.

Ask yourself:

i) What have I learned about myself? Identify key areas where you've grown and areas that still need attention.

ii) What changes can I make moving forward? Develop a plan to continue enhancing your emotional intelligence based on the insights you've gained.

Tip: Schedule regular check-ins with yourself to revisit these steps, ensuring continuous growth in your emotional intelligence journey. Adjust your strategies as needed, and remain committed to your development.

Chapter 25: Building a Strong Social Circle for Sufficient Emotional Support

If you've ever experienced being the life of the party, with folks eager to hang out with you, then you know what it is like to be popular. However, for many of us (myself included), it can be quite a challenging prospect to surround ourselves with people who genuinely like and support us.

This is especially true if we've gone through something difficult, say, a breakup or a family crisis, or if we're healing from addiction or mental health struggles that make it extra hard to connect with others comfortably.

If the above resonates with you, worry not! Building a positive social circle isn't complicated. It just requires stepping out of your comfort zone and allowing others to get close to you *at their own pace.*

Here are several steps to help you do just that:

5 Steps to Build a Strong Social Circle

Here are five strategies to help you build your social circle, whether you've recently moved to a new city, gone through a separation, or started a new career.

1) Understand your level of extroversion.

Knowing this will help you create a tailored plan for your social connections. If you're more introverted, you may want to focus on building a small, close-knit group of friends. If you're extroverted, you may still want a core group of close friends but may also enjoy having a broader circle of *casual acquaintances*. Be honest with yourself—consider taking a personality assessment[xxx] to guide you.

To add to this, it is crucial that you recognize what kind of social circle truly satisfies you. This aspect is all too often overlooked. The goal isn't to accumulate as many friends as possible but rather to connect with people who share your hobbies, passions, and values, ensuring meaningful relationships. If you are less extroverted, forming too many connections could be overwhelming.

How to Go About This

Think back to a time when you were happy with the number of people in your life, and then aim for a similar balance. Some of us are perfectly happy with just two close friends, a romantic partner, and some family connections. Others may need 10 solid friends, a community group for acquaintances, a romantic partner, and regular interactions with neighbors to feel fulfilled. Try and find the balance that works for you and start there.

2) Develop the capacity to approach new people (and know what to say afterward).

Meeting new people is a valuable skill. Learning to introduce yourself and engage in meaningful conversations is crucial for building new relationships. With enough practice, you'll find yourself with abundant connections, which will give you the opportunity to carefully choose who you want in your life.

Mastering the art of approaching others is an excellent tool in social situations. Get comfortable with saying hello to strangers, sharing stories and anecdotes, opening up, asking for contact information, etc.—these are skills you can easily teach and drill into yourself via practice.

How to Go About This

Practice regularly. Start conversations whenever you're out and about. You can also enroll in specific classes, like improv, or take on a job that requires social interaction and offers training. While books and videos can be helpful, they can also become a way to procrastinate, *so prioritize real-life practice.*

3) Be the kind of person whose company others value.

I don't typically advocate placating others on any level. However, having invested in yourself to grow your emotional intelligence, you may have developed skills or attributes that others value being around.

People should want your company because you are kind and contribute in a positive way. This may include making others feel good, being skilled in a useful way, or deliberately creating a fun atmosphere. Traits like humor, empathy, and resourcefulness are very valuable socially. Are you a good listener, nonjudgmental, loyal, etc.? Do you make people laugh or have connections and events that might interest them? These qualities are assets in a social setting.

How to Go About This

Focus on improving empathy by asking open-ended questions and practicing perspective-taking. For humor, consider taking a stand-up or improv class (seriously!) Also, register for events that interest you, and get a few extra tickets to invite others—many events are free or low-cost!

4) Host Events

Hosting events is an effective way to expand your social circle and foster regular interactions with others. By hosting events, you can invite your friends and encourage them to bring along their own friends, creating opportunities to meet new people.

How to Go About This

This one may look particularly difficult to pull off, but it really isn't. Start by organizing small gatherings at your home or in your backyard. You could set up themed events, like a poker night, a s'mores-making session around the fire pit, a doggy playdate, a pillow fighting event, etc. When you meet new people, you'll have enjoyable events to invite them to. Start with smaller gatherings and build from there.

5) Keep Track of People

Make notes about what you learn about individuals so you can recall and reference these details in future conversations. Record their hobbies, favorite music, activities they enjoy in their free time, preferred foods, favorite movies, sports, books, TV shows, and places they like to visit or shop.

This practice is beneficial for building your social circle because it helps identify common interests, making it easier to keep conversations flowing and engaging. People will appreciate that you've taken the time to understand their hobbies and interests. Doing this also provides excellent reasons to reach out, such as when something reminds you of them or if you have a follow-up question about a previous discussion.

How to Go About This

Leverage technology to keep track of these details. Use your phone to make notes, create a spreadsheet, or employ a CRM tool[xxxi]. You may even consider using voice recorders. Don't hesitate to step away briefly during or after a conversation to jot down information that you deem important, if you won't remember it on your own.

Conclusion

This book aims to be a comprehensive manual on emotional intelligence. We've covered pretty much every aspect and element of EQin a fashion that is easy to digest for everyone.

However, it is one thing to read and internalize and a different one to actually apply the wisdom that you've picked up. As such, I want you to be truly intentional in your application of everything that you have learned here. And don't wait for tomorrow, or next week, etc. *Start today.* Begin working on improving your empathy levels immediately, cultivating emotional resilience, applying yourself in an emotionally intelligent manner in your romantic relationship, friendships, etc. And make sure that you assess your progress using the self-assessment exercise we've outlined in the appendix to follow.

Lastly, *knowledge is power*. The more material you read on emotional intelligence, the more emotionally intelligent you will become. So, read as much as possible on the subject to supplement everything you've learned here.

Godspeed!

Appendix

The Emotional Intelligence Self-Assessment Test

This self-assessment test is designed to help you evaluate your emotional intelligence (EQ) across key areas: emotional awareness, emotional regulation, empathy, social skills, and motivation. Each section contains a series of statements.

Rate yourself honestly on each statement using the following scale:

1. **Never**

2. **Rarely**

3. **Sometimes**

4. **Often**

5. **Always**

Section 1: Emotional Awareness

1.   I can easily identify the emotions I am feeling at any given moment.

2.   I understand why I am feeling a certain way in most situations.

3. I am aware of how my emotions impact my thoughts and behaviors.

4. I notice when my mood changes throughout the day.

5. I can distinguish between different emotions I experience, even if they are similar.

Section 2: Emotional Regulation

1. I can calm myself down when I am upset or stressed.

2. I maintain control of my emotions in challenging or frustrating situations.

3. I avoid impulsive reactions, even when I feel strong emotions.

4. I can shift my mood when I need to focus or be productive.

5. I recover quickly from emotional setbacks or disappointments.

Section 3: Empathy

1. I can easily recognize when someone else is feeling upset, even if they don't say anything.

2. I often consider how others might be feeling before I speak or act.

3.	I try to understand situations from other people's perspectives.

4.	I am good at sensing the emotions of those around me, even if they are subtle.

5.	I am compassionate and often offer support to those who are struggling emotionally.

Section 4: Social Skills

1.	I find it easy to build rapport with others in social situations.

2.	I can navigate conflicts or disagreements without damaging relationships.

3.	I communicate effectively and clearly, even in difficult conversations.

4.	I collaborate well with others and often take the lead in group settings.

5.	I influence and inspire others through my words and actions.

Section 5: Motivation

1.	I set challenging personal goals and work diligently to achieve them.

2.   I stay positive and motivated, even when faced with obstacles.

3.   I am driven by a desire to improve myself and grow emotionally.

4.   I am persistent in pursuing my goals, even when progress is slow.

5.   I regularly reflect on my achievements and set new goals for personal development.

Scoring Your Assessment

For each section, calculate your score by summing the numbers corresponding to your responses:

- **21-25**: **High:** You have a strong ability in this area of emotional intelligence.

- **16-20**: **Moderate**: You are doing well but may benefit from further development in this area.

- **11-15**: **Low**: This area may need significant attention and improvement.

- **5-10**: **Very Low**: This area of emotional intelligence may be challenging for you and require focused work.

Interpreting Your Results

1. **Emotional Awareness**: A high score here indicates a strong understanding of your own emotions and their impact on your life. If you scored lower, consider practicing mindfulness and journaling to increase your emotional self-awareness.

2. **Emotional Regulation**: A high score suggests you can effectively manage your emotions, even in difficult situations. If your score is low, you might benefit from learning stress management techniques or practicing emotional resilience.

3. **Empathy**: A high score in empathy means you are likely very attuned to the emotions of others and can connect with them on a deep level. A lower score may indicate the need to practice active listening and perspective-taking.

4. **Social Skills**: High scorers in social skills are often good communicators and can manage relationships well. If you scored lower, you might want to work on improving your communication and conflict-resolution abilities.

5. **Motivation**: A high score in motivation suggests that you are driven and maintain a positive outlook, even when challenges arise. A lower score may indicate the

need to set clearer goals and develop strategies to stay motivated.

Subsequent Steps

Use the results of this self-assessment to identify areas where you excel and areas that may need improvement. Consider setting specific goals to enhance your emotional intelligence (for instance, practicing mindfulness to improve emotional awareness or seeking feedback to understand your empathy levels better.) Also, regularly revisit this assessment to track your progress and continue your journey toward greater emotional intelligence.

Extra Reading for You: Books that will Help You Further Enhance Your Emotional Intelligence

1) *"Emotional Intelligence 2.0" by Travis Bradberry and Jean Greaves*[xxxii] – Offers practical strategies for developing emotional intelligence and improving interpersonal skills.

2) *"The Emotional Intelligence Quick Book" by Travis Bradberry and Jean Greaves*[xxxiii] – Provides an accessible introduction to emotional intelligence and includes practical tips for applying EI concepts.

3) *"Daniel Goleman's Emotional Intelligence: Why It Can Matter More Than IQ" by Daniel Goleman*[xxxiv] – Explores the concept of emotional intelligence and its impact on personal and professional success.

4) *"The Language of Emotions: What Your Feelings Are Trying to Tell You" by Karla McLaren*[xxxv] – Offers insights into understanding and working with your emotions to enhance emotional intelligence.

5) *"Raising Emotionally Intelligent Children: The Heart of Parenting" by John Gottman*[xxxvi] – Provides strategies for parents to help their children develop emotional intelligence.

6) *"Dare to Lead: Brave Work. Tough Conversations. Whole Hearts." by Brené Brown*[xxxvii] – Focuses on building leadership skills through emotional intelligence and vulnerability.

7) *"The Power of Emotional Intelligence: Mastering the Mindset and Emotions that Create Unstoppable Success" by Michael J. J. O'Neil*[xxxviii] – A practical guide to leveraging emotional intelligence for success.

8) *"Emotional Agility: Get Unstuck, Embrace Change, and Thrive in Work and Life" by Susan David*[xxxix] – Offers strategies for managing emotions effectively and adapting to change.

9) *"The Art of Empathy: A Complete Guide to Life's Most Essential Skill" by Karla McLaren*[xl] – Explores empathy as a key component of emotional intelligence and provides techniques for developing it.

10) *"Self-Compassion: The Proven Power of Being Kind to Yourself" by Kristin Neff*[xli] – Focuses on self-compassion as a foundation for emotional resilience and intelligence.

[i] https://journals.sagepub.com/doi/10.2190/DUGG-P24E-52WK-6CDG

[ii] https://www.verywellmind.com/iq-or-eq-which-one-is-more-important-2795287

[iii] https://www.mentalhealth.org.uk/explore-mental-health/a-z-topics/physical-health-and-mental-health#:~:text=Our%20bodies%20and%20minds%20are,an%20upset%20stomach%2C%20for%20example.

[iv] https://www.who.int//news-room/questions-and-answers/item/stress/?gad_source=1&gclid=Cj0KCQjw2ou2BhCCARIsANAwM2HgZZYQ5pDzrxffAYpkf2uBzp06mchJNNHWzjN2Jg1oZgq8aikHPzAaAgwKEALw_wcB

[v] https://www.ncbi.nlm.nih.gov/pmc/articles/PMC4525433/

[vi] https://www.ncbi.nlm.nih.gov/books/NBK537064/

[vii] https://www.ncbi.nlm.nih.gov/pmc/articles/PMC10490081/#:~:text=Finally%2C%20eating%20can%20affect%20one's,may%20eventually%20lead%20to%20depression.

[viii] https://newsinhealth.nih.gov/2018/02/power-pets#:~:text=Interacting%20with%20animals%20has%20been,support%2C%20and%20boost%20your%20mood.

[ix] https://www.ncbi.nlm.nih.gov/pmc/articles/PMC10410209/

[x] https://www.researchgate.net/publication/6795222_Human_Empathy_Through_the_Lens_of_Social_Neuroscience

[xi] https://iep.utm.edu/theomind/

[xii] https://www.sciencedirect.com/topics/neuroscience/brain-activation#:~:text=In%20humans%2C%20the%20face%20motor,1999%3B%20Papathanassiou%20et%20al.%2C

[xiii] https://www.sciencedirect.com/science/article/pii/S1878929324000276#:~:text=Together%2C%20findings%20in%20adults%20suggest,in%20the%20theta%20frequency%20range.

[xiv] https://www.barnesandnoble.com/w/a-bug-and-a-wish-karen-scheuer/1119379666

[xv] https://www.amazon.com/What-Thought/dp/1936943034#:~:text=Authors%20Amy%20Kahofer%20and%20noted,natural%20wisdom%20and%20healthy%20feelings.

[xvi] https://www.amazon.com/Duck-Rabbit-Amy-Krouse-Rosenthal/dp/0811868656

[xvii] https://www.amazon.com/Stand-My-Shoes-Learning-Empathy/dp/1935326457

[xviii] https://www.amazon.com/The-Weird%2521-Series-3-book-series/dp/B078MLTNHM

[xix] https://www.amazon.com/Hey-Little-Ant-Phillip-Hoose/dp/1883672546

[xx] https://www.radicalcandor.com/blog/a-big-change-for-candor-inc/

[xxi]

https://www.researchgate.net/publication/318586397_The_positive_and_negative_psychology_of_empathy

[xxii]

https://www.researchgate.net/publication/310839001_Empathy_by_dominant_versus_minority_group_members_in_intergroup_interaction_Do_dominant_group_members_always_come_out_on_top

[xxiii]

https://www.researchgate.net/publication/47544155_Social_Class_Contextualism_and_Empathic_Accuracy

[xxiv] https://psychcentral.com/health/emotion-wheel

[xxv] https://www.webmd.com/balance/stress-management/stress-relief-breathing-techniques

[xxvi] https://www.lean.org/lexicon-terms/5-whys/#:~:text=5%20Whys%20is%20the%20practice,working%20(Ohno%201988%2C%20p.

[xxvii] https://www.nimh.nih.gov/health/topics/caring-for-your-mental-health

[xxviii] https://brenebrown.com/about/

[xxix] https://www.eitrainingcompany.com/eq-i/

[xxx] https://www.truity.com/test/big-five-personality-test

[xxxi] https://keap.com/product/what-is-crm

[xxxii] https://www.amazon.com/Emotional-Intelligence-2-0-Travis-Bradberry/dp/0974320625

[xxxiii] https://www.amazon.com/Emotional-Intelligence-Quick-Book/dp/0743273265

[xxxiv] https://psycnet.apa.org/buy/2013-17079-001

[xxxv] https://www.amazon.com/Language-Emotions-Karla-McLaren-ebook/dp/B003X27LCM

[xxxvi] https://mindsinactioncounseling.com/emotionally-intelligent-children-and-the-role-of-validation/

xxxvii https://www.amazon.com/Dare-Lead-Brave-Conversations-Hearts/dp/0399592520

xxxviii https://www.amazon.com/power-emotional-intelligence-Harnessing-Emotions/dp/B0BYGT972Y

xxxix https://www.amazon.com/Emotional-Agility-Unstuck-Embrace-Change/dp/1592409490

xl https://karlamclaren.com/product/the-art-of-empathy-a-complete-guide-to-lifes-most-essential-skill/

xli https://www.amazon.com/Self-Compassion-Proven-Power-Being-Yourself/dp/0061733520

Made in United States
Troutdale, OR
04/14/2025